HOME TEAM

SEAN PAYTON

AND **ELLIS HENICAN**

HOME TEAM

COACHING THE SAINTS AND NEW ORLEANS
BACK TO LIFE

 NEW AMERICAN LIBRARY

NEW AMERICAN LIBRARY
Published by New American Library, a division of
Penguin Gro up (USA) Inc., 375 Hudson Street,
New York, New York 10014, USA
Penguin Group (Canada), 90 Eglinton Avenue East, Suite 700, Toronto,
Ontario M4P 2Y3, Canada (a division of Pearson Penguin Canada Inc.)
Penguin Books Ltd., 80 Strand, London WC2R 0RL, England
Penguin Ireland, 25 St. Stephen's Green, Dublin 2,
Ireland (a division of Penguin Books Ltd.)
Penguin Group (Australia), 250 Camberwell Road, Camberwell, Victoria 3124,
Australia (a division of Pearson Australia Group Pty. Ltd.)
Penguin Books India Pvt. Ltd., 11 Community Centre, Panchsheel Park,
New Delhi - 110 017, India
Penguin Group (NZ), 67 Apollo Drive, Rosedale, Auckland 0632,
New Zealand (a division of Pearson New Zealand Ltd.)
Penguin Books (South Africa) (Pty.) Ltd., 24 Sturdee Avenue,
Rosebank, Johannesburg 2196, South Africa

Penguin Books Ltd., Registered Offices:
80 Strand, London WC2R 0RL, England

Published by New American Library, a division of Penguin Group (USA) Inc. Previously published
in a New American Library hardcover edition.

First New American Library Trade Paperback Printing, August 2011
10 9 8 7 6 5 4 3 2 1

New American Library Trade Paperback ISBN: 978-0-451-23337-0

The Library of Congress has catalogued the hardcover edition of this title as follows:
Payton, Sean
  Home team: coaching the Saints and New Orleans back to life/Sean Payton and Ellis Henican.
    p. cm.
  ISBN 978-0-451-23261-8
  1. Payton, Sean. 2. Football coaches—United States—Biography. 3. New Orleans Saints
(football team) 4. Football—Social aspects—Louisiana—New Orleans. 5. Hurricane Katrina,
2005.
  GV939.P388A3 2010
  796.332'640976335—dc22   2010013731

Printed in the United States of America

Set in Sabon
Designed by Pauline Neuwirth

For those who came while others were leaving:
Beth, Meghan and Connor,
the coaches, players and staff of the New Orleans Saints
and all the brave and generous souls
who've helped to revive
New Orleans and the Gulf Coast—
my home team

▪ CONTENTS ▪

▪ CONTENTS ▪

HOME TEAM

▪ INTRODUCTION ▪

WHEN THEY REALLY LOVE you in New Orleans, they have their own unique ways of saying so. If a great trumpet player dies, people don't get all mournful. They dance in the streets with brightly colored umbrellas, then slide the dearly departed into a concrete tomb a couple of feet off the ground.

Well, I'm not ready for my own jazz funeral. Not yet. But I'm pretty sure I have now experienced the next-best thing: riding down St. Charles Avenue on a giant Mardi Gras float, parading with a bunch of guys I love and admire and some of the hottest brass bands on Earth while hundreds of thousands of appreciative people yell, clap, cheer, wave signs, weep openly and call out our names.

They were cheering for their team.

They were cheering for their city.

They were cheering for themselves.

And we were cheering right back at them.

How many people turned out for the New Orleans Saints Super Bowl Victory Parade? Nobody knows for certain. Attendance isn't taken at Mardi Gras parades. Eight hundred thousand? The media estimates went as high as a million. Either way, that's really saying something in a city whose official population is in the mid-300,000s, down a quarter since Hurricane Katrina, a metro area of a million and low change. Basically, nobody stayed home.

I know what I saw from my float as we inched through the crowds: men, women and children, fifteen and twenty deep, a swirling sea of black and gold along the entire 3.7-mile route from the Louisiana Superdome through the Central Business District, out and back down Canal Street, to Mardi Gras World on the Mississippi River.

"Thank you!" they screamed.

"We're back, baby!"

"New Aaaaw-lins!"

New Orleans may not be the swiftest when it comes to amassing Super Bowl victories. But let me tell you: This city knows how to throw a parade. It was hard to imagine anything like this in any other city, this category 5 outpouring of gratitude and love. Babies in tiny Saints hats, giggling and waving. Grown women shouting the universal Saints hello: "Who dat? Who dat?" Burly men hugging one another. Kids rushing up for autographs. One old man in a Deuce McAllister jersey was standing by a blue police barricade on Howard Avenue, tears running down his face. Three Catholic nuns at Canal and Baronne were so ecstatic they were jumping up and down.

These were the people we'd been playing for—people who'd lost so much and struggled so valiantly, literally crying tears of joy. They'd lived though unthinkable hardship: losing their homes, being scattered across the country, some of them seeing their relatives drown. They came from every neighborhood and every background. Relative newcomers and people whose families have been in Louisiana for centuries. Black people. White people. People in such elaborate costumes, you couldn't tell who they were. All of them were united in triumph now.

Many had brought signs from home. These weren't pre-printed placards. These were handwritten sentiments, direct and personal. "Bless you, Boys!!" "Only yo mama loves you more than we do!" "Our City, Victims to Victors." "Baylen Brees, will you marry me?" Baylen is Drew's baby son.

These were the people Jimmy Buffett was talking about when he called New Orleans "the soul of our country." They have been so kind to us. I truly have come to treasure them.

The people of this region lived through the most devastating natural disaster in American history. Eighty percent of their city was flooded when the levees broke. They'd lost their jobs. People they'd known, people they loved had been forced to leave and weren't coming back. Government had failed them at every level. The media had grown bored and moved on. And yet these people still had not lost their will to celebrate. Their spirit made me care deeply about a place I had barely known before. Their courage inspired a struggling football team all the way to the Super Bowl.

And here they were, standing shoulder to shoulder on this raw New Orleans night. Everything in New Orleans gets a name in a hurry. This was either Dat Tuesday or Lombardi Gras. Clearly, we were all locked together, city and team.

Reggie Bush looked totally Hollywood in dark sunglasses and a thousand-watt grin, throwing black-and-gold Saints beads and stuffed minifootballs from the running backs' float. He and Pierre Thomas shared a microphone—and some impromptu raps for the crowd. Tough-guy tight end Jeremy Shockey turned suddenly bashful as people started chanting his name. Darren Sharper, Tracy Porter and others from the secondary rode a float with a pirate theme. That seemed right, given how often they ended up stealing the

other team's ball. Thomas Morstead and Garrett Hartley—
our young punter and young kicker, whose combined ages
added up to mine—rode on a float borrowed from the all-
female Krewe of Muses. Appropriately, it featured a giant
shoe. Garrett kept jumping off the float, hugging and high-
fiving the people he passed.

Tom Benson, the team's eighty-two-year-old owner, was the
first to reach historic Gallier Hall, where the local politicians
were waiting with elaborate champagne toasts. "Hail, Saints!
Hail, Saints! Drink up!" Mayor Ray Nagin called out.

"This win is for the people of New Orleans and Louisiana,"
Mr. Benson said.

A grinning Drew Brees, our phenomenal quarterback and
the Super Bowl MVP, rolled through the streets surrounded,
as he often is, by his offensive line. Their float had a giant
head of Bacchus, the Roman god of drinking and wine.
Drew was tossing so many minifootballs, some people in the
crowd grew alarmed: Was he putting his carefully repaired
shoulder at risk? But Drew was feeling no pain. On this
night, the deadly accurate passer, who'd hit a record thirty-
two of his thirty-nine Super Bowl attempts, was aiming—oh,
just anywhere.

"How's the Who Dat Nation feel tonight?" he called out
to the screaming crowd, his question greeted with a giant
roar. "New Orleans, we love you, baby!"

I rode with my assistant coaches on a "Smoky Mary"
superfloat borrowed from the Krewe of Orpheus. Joe Vitt
and Gregg Williams and Pete Carmichael and Big Dan Dalrymple and the others. I wanted all of them there. My wife,
Beth, rode too. So did our children, Meghan and Connor. I
believe in making these things a family affair. After what my

family had been through with me, they deserved this ride at least as much as I did.

But the star of our float was the Vince Lombardi Trophy. I'd had the trophy with me since Sunday night in Miami when NFL commissioner Roger Goodell handed it to Mr. Benson and he handed it to me. The trophy is a regulation-size, sterling-silver Tiffany football in the kicking position. It is the most prestigious prize we have in our game—something most New Orleans Saints fans had never expected to see up close. I'd gotten some grief in the media for admitting I'd slept with the trophy the night we won. More like I'd passed out next to it. I'd even joked that I might have drooled on Vince. You know what? Maybe I did. But now, here I was, standing in front of this roaring crowd, holding this seven-pound piece of hardware over my head, hugging it, kissing it, waving it and shaking it for the crowd, pumping the trophy in the air. People understood immediately what it meant. It was an amazing symbol of triumph over adversity, a reminder of how far this team and this city had come. I wanted everyone to get a piece of that silver football.

When people saw the trophy, it was like they were viewing the Holy Grail. At one point, I got off the float—this was silly of me. But I got off the float because I wanted to get down to the street level and let some people touch it. Just touch it.

As I moved toward the crowd, people were leaning forward and reaching and squealing. In a few seconds, it was like an ant colony, with people just wanting to feel the trophy to know that it was real. For a moment, I disappeared beneath that hill of humanity. Nobody was pushing. Nobody was violent. But I could see the police moving toward me.

They looked a little concerned. They opened up a path and hustled me and the trophy back up to the float.

Whew!

By the time our float reached Gallier Hall, things had gotten so loose, the U.S. Marine Corps Band and the Ying Yang Twins were trying to outdo one another with competing versions of "Stand Up & Get Crunk," the Saints' unofficial Southern-rap anthem. I was seven Bud Lights in. It was my turn to greet the mayor. My wife squeezed my wrist and said, "Control yourself, honey."

In his toast, Mayor Nagin praised the "gazumbas" I'd shown by calling that ambush onside kick to start the second half. *Gazumbas?* Only in New Orleans does a mayor compliment a football coach quite so vividly.

I just smiled.

"We wish all of you could spend one night with this trophy," I said to the crowd. "Your support means so much to us. We thank you, and we'll see you again this time next year."

As the parade rolled on, it was hard to take all of it in. I wanted to embrace this unique moment, to feel it, to inhale it, to record every detail. The noise. The camera flashes. The outstretched hands. The love. Especially the love. I didn't want any of it to end, as a mad jumble of memories rushed furiously around my head.

Playing football in high school and college and dreaming of the pros. Learning that coach—not quarterback—was my best position. Saying "yes" to Bill Parcells, "no" to Al Davis and "oh, well" to Green Bay. Getting my head around the whole idea of New Orleans, then trying to think of an answer when my wife asked me: "Are we really moving this family into a disaster zone?"

Taking over a team the media gave no chance to, whose stadium was an international symbol of misery and might never reopen anyway. Picking schools for the children, finding a quarterback for the team and letting a Heisman-winning running back fall in our laps. Getting into the Dome and packing the place with the loudest and most grateful fans on earth. People who couldn't imagine staying in Houston or Atlanta or some other sensible place.

The buildings in downtown New Orleans are very close to the street, and many of them have second-floor balconies. So even up on a float, you can look directly into the eyes of the people. It's all more intense and personal here. The parade was like four hours of third down and five.

As we snaked through downtown, the adrenaline never let up. These were the people who'd been counting on us to bring a team and a city back to life. I think we both felt some relief.

And what was I doing here? Me. Someone who'd never been a head coach before. Anywhere. Leading a team that usually brought up the rear. A Midwestern kid, a decent college player who'd had a few cups of coffee in the pros but never really gotten a foothold there. A coach with strong feelings, looking for the right place to land. A guy who didn't get his dream job, showing up in a city whose survival was a genuine question mark, and discovering he belongs there.

As I rode in the parade that night, laughing and shouting and waving that trophy around, I knew right then I had to tell this story. I had to tell it as well as I could.

How a city and a team actually rescued each other. How neither one of them could have done it alone.

1

FOOTBALL DREAMS

I COME FROM NAPERVILLE, Illinois, an old farming community that became a prosperous outer suburb of Chicago. The area is known for its high-tech office parks, its educated workforce and its excellent public schools. It is tidy and overwhelmingly white. Naperville has a river, the DuPage. It isn't quite the Mississippi.

Both my parents grew up around Scranton, Pennsylvania, anthracite coal country, although I was actually born in San Mateo, California. I was the third of four children with two sisters and a brother. My dad worked in insurance. He moved the family a couple of times. But Naperville is where I went to junior high and high school. It's where I learned to love the game of football.

I went out for the team at Naperville Central High. Go, Redskins—excuse me, Redhawks! No one would call me an instant standout. I mostly sat on the bench until senior year.

But I knew every diagram in the playbook, and I loved to analyze game films when I went home at night. Our coach, J. R. Bishop, liked my intensity. My senior year, he made me his starting quarterback. Coach Bishop had a brilliant football mind, especially for the passing offense. For years he ran passing clinics for high school players around the Midwest. To this day, Coach Bishop comes to our training camp every August to be a part of our team. Outside of my parents, he was definitely my biggest influence growing up. He told me I had the talent and the smarts to be a successful quarterback, and he said it with such conviction, I couldn't help but believe him. He trusted me enough to let me call my own plays when we were way ahead late in a game. That's rare in high school. The Redskins were quite a force in the DuPage Valley Conference in the fall of 1981. Our team made it to the play-offs that year. I made enough of an impression that I won a football scholarship to Eastern Illinois University.

I was a better player in college than I was in high school, especially if it had to do with throwing the football. People at Eastern Illinois tell me I had the third-highest passing yardage in NCAA Division 1-AA history: 10,665. I know my seventy-five touchdowns were a school record until Tony Romo sailed past me in 2002. We went 11-2 my senior year.

I loved the whole dynamic of a football offense, predicting where my open receivers would be, scrambling when I had to, counting on the protection of a sturdy offensive line. The quarterback has to account for a large number of variables, working under pressure and making decisions on the fly. Football taught me the thrill of that. But most of all, football gave me confidence and it gave me a goal. After college, I didn't feel done yet. I wanted to make a run at the pros. I knew it wouldn't be easy. Six-foot, 200-pound quarterbacks from Eastern Illinois are not the biggest pro-scout magnet. But I wasn't finished chasing that dream. I knew the odds were against me. I knew it wouldn't be easy. And if, for whatever reason, it didn't work out, I figured I could always do what J. R. Bishop had done: I could be a football coach.

I was a good quarterback. But the truth is, I wasn't good enough to play professionally. Not for a living. At least I was smart enough to figure that out relatively soon. Relatively. The 1987 draft came. I didn't get drafted. I had a one-day tryout with the Kansas City Chiefs. Their quarterback was hurt in a car wreck. I got fifty dollars for the day and a night in the local Adam's Mark. That was my Chiefs career. Someone came up with the idea of playing football indoors. That spring, I tried out for the Chicago Bruisers, one of the original four clubs of the Arena Football League. I made the team and played in a grand total of four games. There was a mixed crew in the league: some ex–NFL players, some first-year guys just out of college like me. After Week Three of the season, we were flying to Pittsburgh to play the Gladiators, when I got a call from Wayne Giordano, general manager of the Ottawa Rough Riders of the Canadian Football League. He wanted me to play for them. This was a step in the right direction—from the small time to the not-quite-as-small time. In one short phone conversation, the Canadian GM and Jim Foster, the Arena owner, made a deal for my football rights: I'd play Friday night's game in Pittsburgh. Then I'd fly to Ottawa. The Rough Riders would pay the Bruisers one thousand dollars to release me. In leagues like these, this is what passes for a big-money deal. For the record, I was the first player ever traded or sold in the Arena Football League.

In my month and a half in Ottawa, I didn't get any playing time. They used me on the practice squad. The coach, Fred Glick, called me into his office one day and said matter-of-factly: "We're moving on." I went back home to Naperville. I painted condos with my buddies and started looking for my next football job. That fall, the NFL players went on strike, and I thought that might be an opportunity. It was, briefly. I caught on as a replacement quarterback with the Chicago Bears—"the Spare Bears," they called us. All the fans wanted to know was, "When are the real Bears coming back?" In three games, I completed eight of twenty-three passes for seventy-nine yards, no touchdowns and one interception. I was sacked seven times for minus forty-seven yards. Numbers like those didn't give the real Bears too much incentive to keep me around when the players' strike ended after twenty-four days. I was clearly running low on options. But I still had one last Hail Mary career move. By the way, that one interception came at the hands of the replacement New Orleans Saints.

You know that John Grisham book *Playing for Pizza*? It's about a quarterback who can't get work in the NFL, so he signs on with a semipro team in Italy. Change a few details, and that was me. Only I went to England instead of Italy. My team was the Leicester Panthers of the UK Budweiser National League. I liked the idea of a beer-sponsored football league, and the Panthers seemed happy to have me. The deal worked like this: They recruited four Americans as player-coaches on what was really one step up from a club team. We got free beer and spending money. The rest of the players were blue-collar British guys who weren't being paid to play American football. They figured at least we knew the game. The four of us played, coached, lived in a house together, lifted weights in the morning, hit golf balls in the afternoon and hung out in the local pubs at night, all with equal vigor. I was single. I was playing the game I loved. I was having the time of my life. I especially took to the coaching part. Working with the Brits during our evening practices. Trying to teach them things I knew about the game. Seeing actual improvement. I got real satisfaction out of that and seemed to have some talent for it.

It was right in that period that the thought finally clarified in my mind. Maybe I wasn't going to be a top-level professional quarterback. But coaching, I decided early that summer, really could be the thing for me. I was also starting to hear stories from my friends back home. They were twenty-two or twenty-three by then. They were buying nice little houses on the outskirts of town. They were starting careers, getting married, having babies and getting on with their lives. I was feeling like I needed to move on. Staying in England forever wasn't much of an option. So how was I going to find a coaching job?

2

COLLEGE DAYS

IT WAS TIME TO return to America.

I remembered from my days at Eastern Illinois that there was such a thing as a graduate assistant in a college football program. The assistants weren't full-time coaches. But they would pass out rosters, edit film and perform any other tasks the coaches told them to. This was the entry level, the absolute ground floor of the college coaching world. It wasn't even officially a job. Instead of a salary, the graduate assistants got grad school tuition and room and board. These positions were still hard to get. But if you got one and caught the eye of the real coaches on your staff, maybe they'd hire you eventually as an actual assistant—or recommend you to one of their coaching friends. It definitely sounded better than painting condos in Naperville.

Still in England, I heard about an opening for a graduate assistant at the University of Nevada at Las Vegas. But to have any chance of being chosen, I'd have to go for an interview with Coach Wayne Nunnely within the week. Getting from Leicester to Las Vegas is easier said than done. And expensive, I might add. I bought a two-day round-trip ticket from a travel agent for £980, which was pretty much all the money I had, and I went to see Coach Nunnely. He was a heavyset fellow I'd never met before. We had a nice talk. As we were finishing, he said, "I gotta ask you one question, and I want your honest answer."

OK.

"If one of the coaches on our staff ever asked you to do something and you thought maybe it wasn't right or maybe it wasn't ethical, what would your reaction be?"

A thought went racing through my head. *Man, these Vegas guys are cheating. He's asking me if I'd be loyal if they hired me.*

"Coach," I said, "I'll be honest with you. If I'm working for your staff, I'm going to do what your staff asks. So regardless what they ask of me, I'm gonna do it with blinders on and not really hesitate."

Coach Nunnely paused. There was quiet in the room. It was just the two of us. "Wrong answer," he said. "I would want you to come to me."

Uh-oh.

I tried to salvage my calculated answer. "Certainly I would come to you," I said. "When you asked that question, I thought you wanted to make sure I was someone who would do whatever was asked of him. I would always want to be thought of that way. Loyal."

"I can appreciate that," the coach said.

The day after I landed back in England, I got the follow-up

call from Las Vegas. They'd hired some other young guy. I hated to hear that. But I learned a lesson early that has stuck with me my entire coaching career: Don't just tell people what you think they want to hear. Take the time to figure out what you really believe. I hadn't done that the way I should have, and it probably cost me.

But that wasn't the end of that. Three days later, I got a call from Steve Devine, the offensive line coach at San Diego State. He supervised their graduate assistant program. He said he'd been speaking with Wayne Nunnely in Las Vegas. He'd also heard about me from Jim Wachenheim, who'd been one of J. R. Bishop's assistants in Naperville and was then coaching at University of the Pacific. They'd both said I might be looking for a GA position. That's another lesson I was learning in a hurry. Coaching is a small fraternity. People talk. Relationships matter. Take good care of them.

I told Steve Devine I didn't have any money left to fly to California for an interview. I'd spent it all traveling to Las Vegas. But we talked on the phone a while, and then he said: "We need three GA's. You've gotten good recommendations. So do you want to accept this position with San Diego State? We'll need you here August first."

And just like that, my football coaching career had begun. God, I had so much to learn. I flew from London to Chicago, gathered my stuff and drove three days to San Diego in a brown 1980 Chevy Cavalier that broke down in Denver. I really felt I was onto something here.

In San Diego, I got busy trying to make a good impression. Denny Stolz, the head coach, thought I worked hard, and I did. As a graduate assistant, you're really competing with the other GA's on the staff for the attention of the head coach. In college football he is unquestionably the boss. I worked with the offense. I spliced tape. I almost never went home, and that's no exaggeration. I had a little army cot in the office, and I slept there for a while. It was doable. They had showers and a steam room and toiletries—everything you'd need. I stayed in San Diego for two seasons. Not a bad place to be a single, aspiring coach.

This wasn't a big start, but it was a real one. I was on my way into coaching. From San Diego, I worked my way up the college football world. I got a full-time assistant's job at Indiana State—$22,500, health insurance and a state-owned car with a sycamore leaf on the side. I was assigned to work with the quarterbacks and receivers, and I had my own recruiting area. I'd met the head coach, Dennis Raetz, when I was in college and he'd come to Eastern Illinois to watch the St. Louis Cardinals practice. He'd remembered me. It was at Indiana State that I started to learn what life is really like as an assistant college football coach. Let's just say that in the early years, glamorous is not quite the word.

Indiana State is also where I met a young woman from tiny Morocco, Indiana, named Beth Shuey. She had just graduated with a marketing degree and moved to Indianapolis for a job in business sales. She was beautiful. She was smart. She at least pretended to be interested in my theories about next year's Sycamore offense. She had no problem with my Dockers-and-red-flannel wardrobe. She was OK with the $22,500. God only knows why she was attracted to a young football coach with too much intensity and a desire to move every year or two. Maybe it was the cool sycamore leaf on the side of my car. We dated. That meant plenty of one-hour drives down I-70 between Terre Haute and Indianapolis. We got married. Could she have possibly known what she was in for? There's an expression in our business about outkicking your coverage. Clearly, I had done that with Beth. When I was asked to return to San Diego State, this time as a real assistant coach working with the running backs, she said, "Let's go." After a lifetime of Midwestern winters, she said Southern California sounded just fine to her.

No one ever gets a college coaching job from a newspaper ad. As you're building a coaching career, one job leads to another, almost always with someone who knows you from someplace else. Your schools might be bitter rivals, but the man on the other sideline—or the guy in the headset barking orders beside you—is often the one recommending you for your next coaching position. It's a very small world out there. Everybody knows everybody. Your reputation is all you've got.

And if you want to advance, be ready to keep moving.

We spent two years in San Diego. Then it was on to Miami University in Oxford, Ohio, with Randy Walker. I was the quarterbacks coach. Then a year at the University of Illinois. Beth and I bought our first house in Champaign.

This is a crazy life, jumping from college to college like that. It's almost like being in the Army. It's especially hard on young families. There's a reason so many get out of the profession to sell insurance or coach high school ball. From San Diego to Indiana back to San Diego to Ohio to Illinois— none of these jobs was easy. None of them was especially well paid. But I loved every one of them. I was learning more about the game of football. I was learning how to motivate. And I was meeting a group of fellow coaches who would become my colleagues and good friends. Many would later join me for our Super Bowl run in New Orleans.

Those were glorious times. Driving a U-Haul to Ohio, pulling Beth's Mitsubishi Galant. The university couldn't pay to move us, but they gave us a BP credit card. We'd fill the tank, then stock up on candy, chips, sandwiches, drinks and anything else they sold in the service-station mini-mart.

I remember six of us riding in a van from Terre Haute to New Orleans for my very first coaching convention—no idea the city would ever be anything but a party town to me. We shared a two-bed room at the Holiday Inn on Bourbon Street. First four guys in at night got bed space. The last two were on the floor.

This is what it's like building a college coaching career. Living in all these different places. Meeting great people who will stay in your life. Storing up the crazy anecdotes.

I remember being in New Orleans one other time with my coaching buddies in those years. After a Superdome barbecue with the Saints, a stop at Pat O'Brien's dueling-pianos bar and a riverboat casino ride, I got a six thirty a.m. call from Lou Toepper, who was head football coach at the University of Illinois. He was in the hotel lobby and just wanted to say hi.

"Did he smell the alcohol on your breath?" Beth wanted to know when I made it back to the room.

"No, I think the gum worked."

I remember, before I left Illinois, sitting with Beth at a basketball game in Assembly Hall. I had a sixty-thousand-dollar contract by then. We were in our midcourt seats. I looked at Beth. She looked at me. I knew what she was thinking. I was thinking it too. "Man, we got it made." She's from Morocco. I'm from Naperville. "We're at the University of Illinois. We're Big 10 now."

In all, I spent nine years as a college football coach. It was really football college for me.

I thought my next stop was going to be the University of Maryland. And it was, briefly. I moved to College Park while Beth was pregnant with Meghan. The plan was to sell the house in Champaign, put the dog in the car and have the baby at our new home in Maryland.

But life throws you surprises. The NFL was never a career goal of mine. Being a head coach at a major university was. In 1997, that changed.

Just as we were preparing to buy a new home in Maryland, the Philadelphia Eagles offered me a job. Our stuff was already packed. The moving van took a left at I-95. Instead of unloading in College Park, Maryland, it headed for South Jersey instead.

This was major.

3

GOING PRO

BY THE TIME I got to Philadelphia, I knew pretty much everything I needed to know about coaching football. At least I thought I did. I was young. I was brash. I'd had successes and failures. I'd worked for some first-rate college coaches and learned lessons from all of them. At this point I figured all I needed was the brighter lights of a bigger stage. The fame, the riches, the accolades—wouldn't they all be mine?

I was clueless.

I was the Eagles' quarterbacks coach, working with offensive coordinator Jon Gruden and offensive line coach Bill Callahan. This was football on a different level, advanced training for me. When I had interviewed with Jon and Bill, Bill said they were looking for "blank tape," an assistant who would keep his mouth shut, listen and learn. Every day, I learned something new from these two or corrected something I learned incorrectly in my previous nine years as a coach. I thought I had worked hard in college. The demands were so much greater in the NFL. Some weeks during the season, I barely went home at all. It was like I was back in San Diego again, just getting started.

Gruden, whose dad had coached at Notre Dame, was one of the brightest young coaches in the league. He'd been with Mike Holmgren in San Francisco and Green Bay and was an expert at the West Coast offense that Bill Walsh had pioneered with quarterbacks Ken Anderson and Joe Montana. Gruden had what we call a very impressive coaching tree. Traditional football theory said establish your running game first, drawing the defense in and opening passing possibilities downfield. The Walsh-Holmgren-Gruden approach said no. You're better off with short passes to the left and right, stretching the defense out. That will open holes for longer running plays. It's faster, bolder and more dramatic than the traditional way football was always played. It also seemed to fit my personality. But after I'd been in Philly a year, Gruden was hired by Al Davis as head coach of the Oakland Raiders. He took Callahan along as offensive coordinator. The head coach in Philly, Ray Rhodes, lasted one more season until he got fired, which meant I was getting fired, which meant here I was looking for a job again.

Yes, insecurity is a fact of life in the pros too.

Philly wasn't a long stay for me, just two years total. But it got me to the NFL. And it gave me two gifts I knew would remain with me the rest of my coaching career: a higher sense of standards and an offensive system that just felt right.

Beth and I drove down to see my mom in Tennessee. My dad had died two years earlier, during my first year in Philly. My mother was living between Nashville and Knoxville in a little place called Fairfield Glade. Jon was trying to get Al Davis to hire me as the Raiders' quarterbacks coach. There were also possibilities with the New York Giants and the Tennessee Titans. I got a message that Jim Fassel, the head coach of the Giants, wanted me to come up to New Jersey and interview for their quarterbacks job. Jon said, "Go interview. I'm still working Al on this end. I don't want you to miss out on something."

The interview with Fassel and his staff went well. After the interview, he offered me the job. It was a good offer, a lot of money for me at the time—a two-year contract: $150,000 the first year, $170,000 the second. I didn't know anyone up there other than Denny Marcin, the defensive line coach, who'd been with me at the University of Illinois. He was the person who recommended me for this position—back to the small coaching fraternity. Gruden was still battling for me in Oakland, but he didn't have a definite yes from Al. So I bought Beth some flowers on the ride home to South Jersey and said, "Hey, you want to go to New York?"

If you asked me, "Where were you put on the map?" I would say, "I was put on the map in New York." And I wasn't the first. Don Shula, Vince Lombardi, Bill Belichick, Tom Coughlin—so many other talented assistant coaches had career stops with the New York Giants. In the movie business, there always seems to be one breakout role where an actor gets spotted. This was going to be that role for me.

I started as quarterbacks coach in 1999 and became the play caller later that season. The following year, 2000, I was promoted to offensive coordinator. That year we had an outstanding season—twelve wins, number one seed and we went to the Super Bowl in Tampa against the Baltimore Ravens.

All of a sudden, I was on the radar.

I was in New York for 9/11. The 2001 Giants opened that season at Denver. It was the first game ever played in the new Mile High Stadium and the first *Monday Night Football* game of the season. September 10, 2001. After the game was over, we flew overnight, west to east, in our United Airlines charter and landed back at Newark about six forty-five a.m. It was Tuesday morning, September 11. As we pulled up in Newark, we didn't know it at the time, but the plane that went down in Pennsylvania was at the gate next to ours. It departed about forty-five minutes after we arrived. So here we are at the gate, and the plane next to ours was the one that would shortly be boarded by the terrorists.

Tuesday was the players' day off. They headed straight home after we landed. The coaches slept on the flight and then went directly to the offices at Giants Stadium in the New Jersey Meadowlands across the Hudson River from downtown Manhattan. Coffee in hand, we began putting a game plan together for the Kansas City Chiefs.

When the planes hit the towers we went up to the top of Giants Stadium. You could see the smoke clearly from there. Beth called to ask if everyone was OK. Then the buildings fell. All of us felt terribly vulnerable that day. At ten thirty that night, as I was leaving the stadium, I saw hundreds of cars in the Meadowlands park-and-ride commuter lot that normally wouldn't be there at that time of night. Some people walked home, up Highway 3 from the city. Many people never made it out of Manhattan that day. The next morning most of those cars were still there.

One of the lessons of 9/11 was that, ready or not, life

went on. We all discovered that living—normally, proudly, unapologetically—was the right thing to do in the face of a terrible threat. Cowering in fear was no answer. For me and the other Giants coaches and the players, that meant returning to the game of football.

2001 turned out to be a .500 season for us. 2002 was my most personally challenging year. We were struggling offensively from the start. In the first three weeks of the season, we were moving the ball effectively. But we weren't scoring enough points.

Week Four of the season, things were going to change. We were playing the Cardinals in Arizona. At the end of the half we got the ball back, deep in our own territory with time for just one play. We were ahead by seven.

"What are you thinking here?" Fassel asked me.

"We should take a knee," I said.

"No, no, let's throw the ball and try to get out of bounds," Fassel said.

"Coach," I answered, "we should take a knee."

Now, Fassel generally gave me complete freedom as a play caller. Nonetheless, we called the pass play. Cardinals defender Justin Lucas intercepted Kerry Collins's pass and returned it for a game-tying touchdown with four seconds left on the clock. The call was obviously a mistake. We had no business running a play like that so late in the half.

God knows I've made my share of bad calls over the years. So I know one when I hear one.

On the bus after the game, I was just sitting there, absorbing the loss, when Beth called. I explained to her what had happened.

"I was listening to the press conference," she said. "They

asked Jim, 'Who made the call at the end of the half?' He said, 'Well, let's just say I gave the green light.'"

That wasn't exactly right. I went in the next day and spoke to Jim.

"Uh, Coach," I said, "whoever takes the blame for that call is unimportant to me. But you know that when we discussed it on the sideline, I said, 'We should take a knee.' You're the one who wanted to run the play. Listen, if you need me to jump on this, I will. But—"

He looked awkward and a little embarrassed. But he couldn't really deny it.

About the same time, I was going through some struggles with my mom. She had just been diagnosed with cancer. After the Rams game in Week Two, I had driven to Nashville. We had won. I brought her the game ball signed by a bunch of the players. I had to tell her she had stage-four cancer. She knew she was sick, but I had to tell her, "This is more serious than we thought." She was a big fighter. She was all gung ho on my bringing her medical reports back to Sloan-Kettering in New York, where the Giants were hooking me up with the best oncologist.

"We'll get all the eyes to look at it," I told her.

The harder message came about three weeks later when the doctors at Sloan-Kettering said, "There's nothing we can do that's different from what they're doing for her in Nashville. The cancer is everywhere."

She deteriorated very quickly. We had a bye in Week Seven. We went down to Tennessee, my siblings and I, to get my mom squared away with in-home care. We got in there on Thursday. By Friday she was in a coma. Friday afternoon, she passed. We buried her on Monday. I went back to New

York the next week. We played the Eagles, a Monday night game. We lost 17-3. Fassel called me in the next day and told me I was no longer going to be calling the plays. He was going to handle it.

"I'm not going to sit still and watch us average one touchdown per game," he told the media. The change he wanted to make was me.

I thought Fassel actually did a great job with the plays. We gained momentum and fought our way into the play-offs. I had another year on my Giants contract. Team officials said they wanted me to stay on in my current role. I had great respect for the owners and for the entire Giants organization. But the head coach and I had such a gap in our relationship, I knew that would be my last year in New York.

To his credit, he made a decision that was hard, and it helped our team. That very same thing happens all the time. I completely respect and grasp and understand the decision. But I really disdained the public ordeal he made of it. Although it ended on a bad note for me, my time in New York with the Giants organization would serve me well later. I remain grateful for the opportunities Jim gave me.

I didn't know it at the time, but there was a guy in Jupiter, Florida, who was paying close attention to all of this. His name was Bill Parcells, the future Hall of Fame coach who had won two Super Bowls with the Giants. Parcells remained close to Chris Mara, whose family founded and continues to own the team. Relationships again. Parcells was going to be the next head coach of the Dallas Cowboys. Chris had told Bill he should hire me if he ever had the chance.

At ten o'clock one night, the phone rang at our house in Northern New Jersey.

"It's Bill Parcells," Beth said.

I'd never met the man before. I knew who he was, of course.

"Hypothetically," Parcells said, "there might be a job that I have an interest in taking." Everyone in New York knew that Bill Parcells had met with Cowboys owner Jerry Jones at nearby Teterboro Airport.

"I may be looking for an offensive coach," Parcells said. "You're someone I might have some interest in visiting with."

4

PROFESSOR PARCELLS

I LOVED WORKING FOR Bill Parcells, and it wasn't just because he brought me to Dallas as his quarterbacks coach after my bad split with Jim Fassel.

Parcells can be ornery. He can be difficult. He isn't always friendly and loose. But Bill Parcells has the best coaching instincts of anyone I've ever worked for. He is gutsy. He is bright. He is inventive. He will take a risk. More important, he knows how to win. All this would become crucial to me when the Saints were going into the Super Bowl. At a time like that, there's no one you'd want to be talking with more than Bill Parcells.

Our personalities are different. I'm more exuberant. He's a little more dour. When I was working for him, he didn't always agree with some of my ideas on offense. But much of my style as a football coach can be traced back to him.

When I went to work for Bill, it wasn't just higher education for me. If Philly and New York had been like going to football college, this was more like enrolling in law school. The professor could be brutal. I had a whole lot to learn. But I would definitely be expanding my mind.

We opened the 2003 Cowboys season with a loss at home to the Atlanta Falcons, 27-13. It was a game we should have won. To call Parcells displeased would be a ten-gallon understatement. He was seething. In the deepest part of his Jersey-born being, he was committed to making sure nothing like that ever happened again. And who did we have waiting for us next? My old buddy Jim Fassel and the New York Giants on *Monday Night Football*. We came from behind to win a game we had no business winning, slipping past the Giants in overtime, 35-32. This was more what Bill had in mind.

I was back in Giants Stadium. It was, "Hi, remember me?" The game also dredged up some nostalgia in Bill. It was his first time back there since he'd coached the Jets and the Patriots. And here's what made the victory even sweeter for both of us: Our team wasn't as good as the team we beat. The Cowboys won because we played harder, played smarter and, yes, were better coached.

Bill helped me understand something that night: It's no great accomplishment to lead the stronger team to victory. The real credit comes when you arrive at a disadvantage—and you still win. That's why the Atlanta defeat was so galling to him and why the New York victory was so sweet.

In the coaches' locker room following the game, Bill was saying what a big win this had been. He turned to me and said: "I know it was especially big for you."

That was the beginning of the end for Jim Fassel, letting Parcells and the Cowboys move past him in overtime like that. Fassel would not be back the following year. And defeating the Giants set a winning tone for the rest of the Cowboys' season.

That first year in Dallas, we won ten games, lost six and went to the play-offs with a very good defense, twice as many victories as the previous year. It was one of Bill Parcells's best coaching jobs ever. It was outstanding. And every step of the way, he was agitated about something. Even after the great victory in the Giants game, he was mad. He'd given his relatives fifteen tickets that night, and they didn't use all the seats. We were on the bus outside Giants Stadium and Bill had a scowl on his face.

"What's wrong?" I asked him.

"They didn't use the seats," he said.

"Coach, we just beat the Giants."

"It's the last fuckin' time I get them tickets. They gave them away. They don't know we paid for those."

I had a great three years in Dallas. I worked with three fine quarterbacks—Drew Bledsoe, Vinny Testaverde and an undrafted kid named Tony Romo, who'd gone to an out-of-the-way school called Eastern Illinois.

But I don't ever remember Parcells being totally satisfied. What I remember is that he never stopped thinking how to win. He said: "You have to look at each game individually and ask yourself: What do we have to accomplish here?" For Bill, fresh analysis beat conventional thinking every time. No preconceived notions. No "We always did it like that before." He was brilliant at analyzing every opponent individually and then figuring out what it would take to win a game. How do we neutralize this team's best players? What weakness of theirs can we exploit? What will they be expecting from us that we will not give them? How do we climb inside their heads—and screw around? Simply put, he knew how to give his team its best chance to win.

If you lost a game 35-30, most coaches would say, "The defense let us down." Bill might get upset at the offense for not scoring the final touchdown—because that's the kind of game it was. If you lost a game 10-7, you would say, "The offense didn't score enough points." Bill might be angry with the defense. "You gave up that field goal!"

He just knew. You have to pay attention to how the game is being played.

He was very confrontational. That was how he grew up. He definitely enjoyed making a point. One thing about Bill: He was able to find out very early who had passion and who did not. If you lacked that passion as a player or a coach, you were probably never going to be a favorite of Bill Parcells. Or mine, as I continued to work with him.

After the opening loss to Atlanta and the win in New York, we won three more games in a row. We were on a roll. We were getting ready to play the Detroit Lions in Week Seven. Most people would have called it the easiest game on the schedule. Bill hated talk like that. He's old school. When you're having success, he is all over you every moment. When you hit a rut, he's building you up. We were playing a team that on paper we were supposed to beat easily. Yet he was on everyone all week: coaches, players, trainers, everyone.

He saw this as a classic trap game. To illustrate his concern, he even had mousetraps hung in the locker room on Wednesday when our players arrived. *"Smack!"* he said, imitating the sound of a mousetrap. He was on the coaches as much as he was on the players. In a coaching staff meeting, he lit into his staff. "This has 'sucker punch' written all over it," he insisted. "You guys aren't ready. Your players aren't ready. You're not focused. We're gonna get our asses kicked."

Everybody was getting sick of it. God, we couldn't wait for this game to come. We went on to beat the Lions handily, 38-7.

Bill understood the power of confrontation, the value of creating a crisis. Most people prefer to be pleasant. Most people would rather get along. But sometimes it really is more valuable to create the crisis, to face the confrontation. That's what Bill did before the Detroit game. On a number of occasions in New Orleans, I would find myself doing much the same thing.

5

MEETING AL

I GOT WORD THAT Al Davis wanted to interview me for the head-coaching job at the Oakland Raiders.

This was after the 2003 season. I'd been in Dallas with Parcells just a year, a year of vast improvement for the Cowboys. But 2003 had been a tough year in Oakland. Their 4-12 record, coming after an 11-4 season in 2002 and a trip to San Diego for the Super Bowl, tied them with the Giants, the Chargers and the Cardinals for the worst in football. As an owner, Al Davis has never been shy about firing his coaches or overruling their decisions. This time, Bill Callahan was the one to pay with his job.

I flew out to Oakland immediately and discovered: There is nothing quite like an Al Davis interview.

One minute, it's defense. The next minute, it's offense. Then it's away-game travel or the off-season program. He never stays on the same subject for very long. He wants to keep you on edge. "Tell me about your thoughts in regard to player tickets. . . . Tell me about your thoughts in regard to team travel. . . . Tell me about your thoughts in regard to your coach's calendar as it pertains to off-season vacation. . . . What kind of defensive front do you think is the toughest to run against? . . . Give me your two best deep passes." Al Davis may have a short attention span. But he's in control of the conversation at all times.

Al is unique among football owners in that he's also been a head coach and a general manager. He was even commissioner of the American Football League. Whatever you think of Al Davis—and people have strong opinions—no one can say the man doesn't know football.

I arrived on Saturday. This was my first interview ever for a head-coaching job. We went well into the night. Around nine thirty California time—it was eleven thirty in Dallas, and I was starving—Al finally said: "Are you hungry?"

"Sure, I'm hungry."

"Jimmy," he called. "Come in here."

A young man appeared. "Mr. Davis, what can I get you?"

"Jimmy," Al said, "we want to get some cheeseburgers." Then, looking at me: "You like cheeseburgers?"

"Sure."

"Can you get us those cheeseburgers and some of the coleslaw they sell with the cheeseburgers?"

Jimmy looked confused. "Mr. Davis," he said, "McDonald's doesn't sell coleslaw. That's Kentucky Fried Chicken."

"Oh, I knew that," Al said. "I knew that. All right, Jimmy. Just get us some of the cheeseburgers."

We continued talking. The assistant disappeared. He came back with a bag of cheeseburgers—not Quarter Pounders with Cheese or Big Macs. The kids-menu cheeseburgers—ten of them. Like the kind that come with the Happy Meal. And then there was another bag of Kentucky Fried Chicken coleslaw.

Al was wearing a black sweat suit and his Super Bowl rings. He was a sloppy eater. He kept a towel in his lap. He was constantly wiping his face on the towel.

We stayed up late that night. The next morning we were up and at it again. And the whole next day. The interview seemed to be going well. The next week, I had a trip planned with my family to Disney World. Al had a couple of other candidates he was interviewing, but he left me with the strong impression that I was high on his list.

"What's your plan?" he asked.

"I'm gonna go back to Dallas," I said. "I'm gonna get the family. I'm gonna be at Disney World in Florida Monday through Sunday, and I'll be available after that. But I planned this trip with the family months ago."

"All right," he said. "I'm gonna be in touch with you. I want you to be thinking about your staff."

When I left Al, I knew I was going to be offered the job. He'd interview a few other candidates. But I'd get the offer.

Now, the whole time, Beth was somewhat guarded. She knows Cindy Gruden. Her husband was in Oakland. She knows Valerie Callahan, Bill's wife. She'd heard their stories about the special challenges of working for Al. All of us were guarded here.

And yet I was driving a hundred miles an hour, passing the "Danger! Falling Rocks!" signs, pedal to the metal, thinking of nothing besides "It's an NFL head-coaching job." I picked the family up in Dallas. We went on to Disney World. And every evening at nine, Al Davis would call. I'd go into the bathroom, close the door and sit on the toilet, and we'd talk about the assistants I wanted to hire. "Who are you interested in?" he'd ask.

Our family had great days together at the theme parks. Then the phone would ring at nine. I'd go back into the bathroom, and there'd be some stress when I came out.

"How did it go?" Beth would ask.

"Well, we were just talking about coaches."

On Wednesday, we were at the Animal Kingdom when Mike Lombardi called. He's Al's general manager. Mike and I had worked together in Philadelphia. "Al wants to speed this thing up and get you out here ASAP," Mike said.

"Mike, it's Wednesday," I said. "I'm here till Sunday."

"I know," Mike said. "But he's adamant that he wants to get this thing going. You've got to call him."

Beth was not happy. "You're not telling me we're going to cut this vacation short?" she asked.

"No," I promised. "I just have to think how I'm gonna present this when I call him."

We were having lunch at the Rainforest Café. Beth, Meghan, Connor and I ordered, and then I said, "Excuse me. I'm gonna go out and make that call."

I sat on a bench beneath a giant mushroom and called Al. "Mr. Davis, it's Sean."

"Hey, Sean," he said. "How are you doing?"

"I'm doing good," I said. "One of the things we talked about last week in the interview process was loyalty and commitment. I know you have a sense of urgency here. But I feel like I've made a commitment to my family that I have to follow up on with this vacation."

"Ah, I understand," he said. "I understand. When can you get back here?"

"Sunday we get back to Dallas," I said. "I can get on a flight to Oakland on Sunday night."

There was relief at the table when I got back. We enjoyed the rest of the week. And Sunday morning, before we flew back home, we set up one of those breakfasts with the Disney characters. Ours was Winnie-the-Pooh.

After breakfast, we checked out of the Disney hotel. We flew back to Dallas. I got the family settled at home and got on a flight to Oakland. Again, Al had dinner brought in. It was sandwiches this time. Breakfast with Winnie, dinner with Al. Just another day in my life.

We didn't leave the complex one time in the five-day interview process. Two days before Disney, three days after. More questions, more topics. Team travel, assistant coaches. "Tomorrow morning when you get in, I want you to look at the St. Louis Rams film against the Carolina Panthers," Al said. "Tell me what you think of that game."

At this point, I was beginning to feel some pressure from Parcells—"Hey, what are you doing? I need to know." And rightfully so: Bill needed to know if I was gone.

"Have you been offered the job?" he asked, direct as ever.

"Coach, I haven't." Not in so many words. Not yet.

The plan was for me to get a flight out of Oakland on Tuesday. "Do you feel good about everything?" Al asked me.

"I do. I just need to get home and talk to my wife."

"Michael's got your agent's name," Al said.

"Great," I said. "I just need to talk to Beth, and you'll have Michael call Don Yee."

By the time I reached the airport, I had five messages from

Parcells. As I walked toward the gate, I saw an ESPN screen with a Raiders logo and my face. "Report out of Oakland is Sean Payton is being hired as the Raiders' new head coach," the anchor said. All of a sudden, Parcells wasn't the only one calling me. My phone was now a constant buzz.

Beth got through. "I thought you said we were going to discuss this," she said.

"We are," I told her.

"Well, I'm seeing where you've been named head coach of the Raiders, or it's imminent," she said.

"There's been no offer," I said. "Honey, I'm on my way. I'm at the airport. I've gotta connect in Denver. I'll be home. We'll discuss it tonight."

"All right," she said.

By the time I changed planes in Denver, the offer had already arrived: a written contract proposal faxed to Don Yee.

When I got back to Dallas, the kids were asleep. Beth and I sat up in bed and talked for two hours.

"This is what they're offering," I told her.

Was it time to leave Dallas? Was I ready as a coach? Was Oakland the place for me? Beth was skeptical. I was skeptical. But I was still driving a hundred miles an hour, trying to keep the skepticism out of my head. When we went to bed Tuesday night, the decision was, "Hey, we're gonna do this." Wednesday, we went out and I bought a black suit with a silver tie for my press conference. When I got to the Cowboys complex Wednesday morning, the equipment guys were packing up my locker and putting my stuff in a box. Bill was in Florida.

I sat at my desk and called my friend Jon Gruden. By then he was head coach in Tampa Bay and knew everything I was weighing. I spoke to John Fox, who was at Carolina, and to Bill Callahan, who was heading to the University of Nebraska, and then the phone rang. It was Parcells. He was calling from Florida.

"Listen," he said. "I want to talk to you for a minute like you were my son. Not like I'm the head coach and you're the assistant."

Our prior discussions had always been coach to assistant.

"These other people that you're close to in the industry, what do they think you should do?" Bill asked.

You have to understand, Bill has a good relationship with Al. So does Jerry Jones, the Cowboys' owner.

"What about Gruden?" Bill asked.

"He doesn't think I should take the job. Absolutely no."

"Fox?"

"He doesn't think I should take the job."

"What about Callahan?"

"He doesn't think I should take the job."

"Well," Bill said, "put my name behind those three. You're gonna get your chance. This isn't the right one, kid."

And we hung up.

In two minutes the phone rang at my desk.

"Sean, this is Jerry Jones. How you doin'?"

"I'm doing well," I told the Cowboys' owner. "Just got back from the interview."

"I know," he said. "Listen, before you tell me anything, I want to visit with you. I'm over at my house. I'll send a driver over. Let's talk a little bit."

"Sounds good," I said.

We sat in the library of Jerry's house in Highland Park. It was just a chat. Not about being persuasive. Just assessing where we were.

He didn't make any commitment about my future if I chose to stay. He didn't name some amount he would pay me. He did not say, "You're going to be the next head coach" or anything like that. What he said was: "I do want you to know we think a lot of you. And should you decide to stay, you've got a bright future here."

If Jerry's the last guy you see before you make a decision, you're probably staying with him. It was very simple: "You're highly thought of in this organization, and I don't want to lose you. But if you go, we'll wish you well."

It was just what I needed to hear. I got in the car to go home. We rode at a normal rate of speed. I called Beth immediately.

"What are you doing?" I asked her.

"Driving the kids," she said.

"Let's stay in Dallas. I don't think I should take this job."

Beth was quiet for a moment, and then she started to cry.

I got back to the office. I called Don Yee. He began to update me on the contract back-and-forth. I stopped him midsentence.

"Get us out," I said. "We're gonna stay in Dallas. For the record, let's not say this job was ever offered."

Don called Oakland. I called Parcells. "Hey, Coach, I'm staying," I said.

I called Jerry Jones. "Mr. Jones," I said, "I appreciate the time today. We're gonna stay in Dallas."

Jerry's son Stephen came to the office. He had a new contract for me. Three years, a million dollars a year. It was absolutely the right decision I made.

I say that with all due respect to the Oakland Raiders and Al Davis, an extremely talented football man. But I don't know truly that I was ready for that job.

Luckily I had two more years with Bill Parcells. That was two more years to learn about football and learn about myself. I was very glad I had that time. When a head-coaching opportunity finally arrived for me, it called on every ounce of strength and experience I could possibly muster. Not only would I be coaching a struggling NFL team, but I'd be doing it under circumstances that no one had ever done it before.

6

MOVE WHERE?

ALL THE BLUE TARPS.

That's what I saw first as the American Airlines flight from Dallas prepared to land at Louis Armstrong International Airport in New Orleans. On the roofs of many of the houses—what was left of them—were these bright blue plastic tarps. They seemed to be covering everything. When I got off the plane, the airport was eerily quiet, almost empty, motionless. It was different from any airport I'd ever seen. You know what it felt like? It felt like they had only one flight a day here, the one I'd just gotten off of. The airport was whatever the opposite of bustling is.

Mickey Loomis, the Saints' general manager, was there to meet me. It was just a ten-minute ride from the airport to the team offices and practice facility on Airline Drive. But as we rode in Mickey's car, the blocks we passed didn't look much busier than the airport. This was early January 2006, four months after Katrina. The floodwaters had finally receded. People were trickling back. But most of the houses still looked empty. The stores and the restaurants were hit-and-miss. Cars were still up on people's lawns. Everything just seemed very still. The grass and the weeds were growing. There were trailers here and there. But you certainly didn't hear a lot of construction noise.

As Mickey and I pulled into the parking lot, I glanced at my cell phone for any sign of a text message or a voice mail from 920, the area code for Green Bay, Wisconsin.

Nothing.

It wasn't like I hadn't heard about Katrina. I'd seen the pictures on television and read the newspaper accounts. I knew about the people on the rooftops and the families in the Superdome. I knew FEMA had stumbled. I knew about the Lower Ninth Ward. I knew the failure of the levees was worse than the storm. But all that media coverage had still failed to prepare me for this: the immensity of the devastation and so much quiet. When I arrived from Dallas for my official Saints interview, New Orleans looked like a third-world country with most of the people gone.

I'd been to the city before. For coaching conventions. For a few games. Always in on a Thursday, out on a Monday, with hardly any rest in between. I always had a great time in New Orleans. But for me, it was one of those cities like Miami or Las Vegas. You were happy to visit, but not in your wildest imagination could you think of living there. And that was *before* Katrina.

After my third season in Dallas with Parcells, I felt like I knew the modern canons of football. I had confidence in my own coaching abilities. I had firm thoughts on how to win. I believed I was ready to coach my own NFL team. Thankfully, some other people agreed. Though I'd stepped back from the Al Davis offer in Oakland two years earlier, now the time seemed right. Several teams were looking for new head coaches in early 2006. I'd flown up to Green Bay and had a terrific interview with the Packers. That's a great organization—a team I had followed since I was a kid. I felt optimistic about that possibility and was expecting to hear something soon. The Buffalo Bills had expressed interest in me as well. I'd also had a nice-to-meet-you dinner with Mickey in San Antonio. Now, with this trip to New Orleans, that preliminary conversation was being elevated to a formal interview.

The Saints were displaced like everybody else in or near New Orleans and the Mississippi Gulf Coast. The day before I got there, the team had returned to Airline Drive from its Katrina-year headquarters in San Antonio. Mickey showed me around the sprawling facility—the indoor and outdoor practice fields, the locker and weight rooms, the executive and staff offices. I could see that plenty of work still had to be done. There'd been damage from the storm and the flooding. The National Guard had used the place as a temporary headquarters. They'd been landing helicopters on the practice field. They treated the offices more like a field command center than an executive suite. The building got three years of wear and tear in three hard months. Clearly, the top-to-bottom fix up still had a ways to go. Walls had to be painted. Carpets had to be pulled. Tarps were hanging everywhere. The furniture was half assembled. As Mickey began to introduce me around, I didn't say anything, but I did think to myself: "They're running an NFL team—from here?"

They'd set up a makeshift meeting area in one of the breakout rooms. Besides Mickey, I met with Greg Bensel, the team's vice president of communications. I saw Rick Mueller and Russ Ball, who'd been at dinner with us in San Antonio and dealt with player-personnel issues. And that afternoon I had a chance to sit down with Mr. Benson. As far as I could tell, no topic was off-limits. I was struck immediately by everyone's openness. The previous season's 3-13 record. The need to hire a new head coach. The unique challenge of rebuilding a football team in a city that itself needed rebuilding. The uncertainty about the team's long-term future in New Orleans.

Visiting with Mr. Benson could not have been more different from my Al Davis interview. No game-day strategies. No run-front defenses. And no cheeseburgers. Mr. Benson asked me about my family and told me about his.

Mickey and the others didn't try to sugarcoat anything. When the storm hit, Mickey told me, he had just laid the foundation for a new house in Metairie. Now he was actually sleeping at the complex. The task at hand was immense. It was all a little surreal, to tell you the truth. And, honestly, I wasn't taking any of it to heart. It just seemed interesting and huge. My basic reaction was: Man, these guys have their hands full! I was most likely going to Green Bay. This was their problem, not mine. I was just here for an interview.

When we finished our various meetings, Mickey drove me downtown to the Renaissance Hotel. At least it was open. I had about an hour and a half to relax before dinner. We were meeting at seven at Tommy's Cuisine. I went up to the room. I took off my coat and loosened my tie. I was relaxing on the bed, almost dozing off. The cell phone began to vibrate. I had a message from 920, Ted Thompson, the Packers' GM. Ted got right to the point. "Hey," he said, "the process has gone well. We've decided to go in a different direction, and I wanted to let you know as soon as possible. It hasn't come out yet. Please don't say anything until we announce it."

I wanted to cry.

I appreciated the heads-up. But damn! I really thought there was a good chance I was getting the Packers job. Without a doubt, Green Bay is where I wanted to go. Knowing the tradition. Coming from the Midwest. Growing up around all that. And Beth too—I knew she could see herself in Green Bay, despite those winters that never end. In that one short voice mail, the Packers job was gone. But I had no chance to reflect on the deeper meaning. It was almost seven. I had just enough time to look in the mirror and straighten my tie. But for the very first time, on my way out to dinner, one thought did creep into my mind. It was more like a sigh followed by a question:

"Oh, man, could I really be going to New Orleans?"

I liked Mickey Loomis from the first time we met. In an industry of loud egos, he had a quieter style. At the time, he'd been with the Saints for six years and before that he'd spent fifteen years with the Seattle Seahawks. He'd worked for successful guys like Chuck Knox and Mike McCormick. I think I have pretty good instincts and intuition. My first impression was dead-on. Trustworthy. Steady. Intelligent. Patient. He was like that in my early meetings with him, and that's how he is today. He has never once glossed over anything.

We talked at dinner about all the issues the Saints would be facing that year and beyond. The issue of getting players to come. The issue of recruiting coaches. All of it was right out on the table. He said, "We've got to discuss this A to Z—all of it." That's Mickey. This was a team that had obviously gone through a lot. They had played their home games in San Antonio, Baton Rouge and East Rutherford, New Jersey. Their stadium was on the injured-reserve list. They had challenges no other NFL team had ever experienced. 3-13 was only the beginning of it. There was just a huge amount of chaos they needed to deal with. Clearly, they had to make a change at quarterback. It was time to move on from Aaron Brooks. And there were real questions about where the team's permanent home would be. They'd be back in New Orleans for the 2006 season, if they had somewhere to play. But how long would the team stay? I don't think anyone had all the answers. Mickey didn't pretend to. He told me what he knew. He told me what he didn't. Sometimes the answer was just: "We'll have to see."

I think Mickey was looking for a head coach who wouldn't be overwhelmed by an extreme situation, someone who might even view it as a challenge to be excited by.

Here's something I noticed as we talked: When we got our salads, I was saying "you" about all the Saints' issues. By dessert, I was mostly saying "we." We could run this kind of offense. We could make a certain trade. We had to do it all amid the post-Katrina turmoil. No job had been offered. No deal had been made. I certainly hadn't discussed any of this with Beth and the kids. I had a pretty good idea of what they might say. But as Mickey and I talked late into the night, with Green Bay now off the table and his frankness washing over me, the first-person plural was definitely creeping into my sentences. I was getting my head around that question

I'd asked myself as I'd left the hotel. Without my even realizing it, an answer was gathering in my mind.

"Maybe yes."

I brought up the idea of my family staying in Dallas and me coming here to work. Mickey wasn't keen on that at all. Whoever came would have to be all in, he said. It was essential that the New Orleans Saints' head coach be as much a part of the team and the community as any player, any team official or any fan. This was not a job a head coach could just phone in.

Before I left New Orleans, Mickey drove me all over the area, everywhere. He showed me the French Quarter, which hadn't flooded and looked relatively normal. We rode through Uptown, with its stately historic homes. But we also drove through Lakeview, Mid-City, the Ninth Ward, New Orleans East—neighborhoods that all had flooded badly, places that four months later still looked like ghost towns. He skirted nothing. As Mickey talked and I was taking it all in, I was already thinking about the next conversation I would have: explaining all this to Beth.

On the flight back to Dallas/Fort Worth, leaving the blue tarps behind, I finally had a few minutes to myself. I'll admit I felt a little excitement about the whole idea of New Orleans. This city and this team needing so much now. What it was I might bring to both of them. If Mickey offered and I said yes, success was certainly not guaranteed. Hell, it might not even be possible. But I knew this much already: It would be the challenge of a lifetime.

I got back to Dallas and sat down with Beth. It was strange. I really hadn't convinced myself yet that New Orleans was a smart idea for us or even doable. And yet I could hear myself trying to sell the idea to my wife. I told her, "This is what I think. Green Bay is going to hire Mike McCarthy. And we're not interested in going to Buffalo. The one thing about New Orleans is it's a fifty-five-minute plane ride from Dallas."

Beth raised an eyebrow. I was waiting to hear her say, "And . . . ?"

We had a great life in Dallas. We had friends and a nice place in the community. We were building a beautiful home. Meghan was almost nine. Connor was almost six. Connor is not big on change, but Meghan also didn't want to leave. She had close friends and loved the school she was in.

Whenever you take a new coaching job and you have a young family, you really spend a year away from them, at least to some degree. You're starting the new job. You have to sell your old house. So you lose a good part of a year. You go ahead and leave. Your wife is left cleaning up the crumbs. And the strongest argument I was making was, "Well, you can fly out of there quickly."

We'd be moving into an area that hundreds of thousands of people had just left. Maybe they left for a reason? Everything was a concern. The crime. Housing. Schools. The medical situation. The basic details of everyday life. We couldn't get rid of those thoughts. And let's be honest: A lot of those things were problems even before Katrina.

We'd always said we were up for an adventure. What an opportunity! What a challenge! What need!

A week passed as we thought through all these issues. There were plenty of them. But Beth and I both gradually began to see that New Orleans actually might be something like a calling for us—a challenge we were meant to take on. I don't believe in destiny. But both of us really did feel that something was pulling us here. Maybe suburban Dallas wasn't the only place we could thrive.

We left it there for the moment. This was all just hypothetical, wasn't it? But that comfort didn't last long. A few nights later, we were at a Bon Jovi concert, Beth and I, at the American Airlines Arena in Dallas. Somewhere between "Living on a Prayer" and "You Give Love a Bad Name," Mickey called. I stepped out to the food court so I could hear. "How'd you like to be head coach of the New Orleans Saints?" Mickey said.

I went back into the arena and looked at my wife. She knew what the call meant. We were going to New Orleans now. It wasn't hypothetical anymore.

The night before the press conference announcing my hiring as the Saints' new coach, I got home and Beth said, "Did you hear what your new mayor said?"

He was *my* mayor now.

"What?"

"You didn't hear?" she said.

"No."

"He said New Orleans has always been a chocolate city," she said. "It's all over the national news."

A what? "You've gotta be kidding me," I said.

Ray Nagin had given a Martin Luther King Jr. Day speech at city hall. He was addressing the city's black residents, who'd long been in the majority. "It's time for us to rebuild a New Orleans—the one that should be a chocolate New Orleans," he said. "And I don't care what people are saying Uptown or wherever they are. This city will be chocolate at the end of the day. This city will be a majority African-American city. It's the way God wants it to be. You can't have New Orleans no other way. It wouldn't be New Orleans."

This is the mayor's idea of promoting harmony on Martin Luther King Jr. Day?

Nagin tried to talk his way out of the uproar, saying he was actually encouraging integration. "How do you make chocolate?" he asked. "You take dark chocolate, you mix it with white milk and it becomes a delicious drink. That's the chocolate I'm talking about."

But that was not exactly how the comment was received by most people, including the Paytons of Dallas, Texas.

As we prepared for the move, clearly, some people in Dallas thought we were nuts. But Cowboys owner Jerry Jones really clarified things for me. This was the last meeting I had with him after I knew I was going to New Orleans. I went in to say good-bye.

"With some of our greatest hurdles come our greatest accomplishments," he said. "As I look back, Sean, some of my greatest achievements have come when I took the most risk."

He talked about going out there and going after something as big as this. "Your reward can be bigger than you ever dreamed," he said.

Big challenge. Big reward.

I didn't know it at the time. I had no idea. But he couldn't have been more right.

7

LOSING TRADITION

I'M NO SAINTS HISTORIAN, which isn't necessarily a bad thing.

But I know this much: On the very first play of the very first game of the very first season of the New Orleans Saints, September 17, 1967, wide receiver John Gilliam returned the opening kickoff ninety-four yards for a touchdown. The sellout crowd at Tulane Stadium went wild.

"Wow, this is easy," local people thought.

But not for long.

The Saints lost that first game, 27-13, to the Los Angeles Rams. And the final score, more than Gilliam's blazing run, set a standard for the expansion team's future. It took another twenty years for the Saints to achieve their first winning season, thirty-three to win their first play-off game.

In fact, New Orleans was lucky to have a National Football League team at all. If it weren't for a Louisiana-style backroom deal in Washington, local football fans would still be making do with Saturday-afternoon keggers before

Tulane and LSU games. In the early 1960s, a New Orleans sports promoter, Dave Dixon, launched a drive to bring professional football to the city. He got big turnouts for a couple of NFL exhibition games. The tourism industry thought the idea was promising. Dixon had undeniable vision and energy. His later projects included the Superdome and the USFL. But the campaign for an NFL team was going nowhere.

League officials thought New Orleans wasn't big enough or modern enough or rich enough to properly support a team. Where were the corporate dollars that would make a franchise thrive? But in 1966, NFL commissioner Pete Rozelle needed something important from Congress.

Rozelle was eager to merge the struggling AFL into his league. But federal antitrust law stood in the way. Rozelle wanted a waiver. The constant bidding wars for college players were getting expensive. The cutthroat competition threatened to bankrupt some teams.

To New Orleans congressman Hale Boggs, Rozelle's obvious eagerness smelled like opportunity.

Boggs was the Democratic majority whip. In a meeting with Rozelle, he made clear that the cost of his vote was a franchise for New Orleans. When the commissioner said, sure, he would definitely work on that, Boggs cut him off immediately—and not in a good way. "Then I guess we're finished here," the congressman said, standing up. Rozelle firmed up his promise on the spot.

"It was definitely a quid pro quo," said Tommy Boggs, the late congressman's son, now a powerful Washington lobbyist.

The House Judiciary chairman, Emanuel Celler, a feisty seventy-eight-year-old from Brooklyn, was a staunch defender of the antitrust law. Boggs needed to neutralize him. So the New Orleans congressman attached the football waiver to a larger bill that was outside the chairman's jurisdiction. Boggs and Louisiana senator Russell Long both got themselves on the House-Senate conference committee. Final approval came October 21.

Rozelle got his waiver. New Orleans got its team. Celler was left shaking his head. "They caught me bathing and sold my clothes," he said.

On November 1, 1966, All Saints' Day, Commissioner Rozelle flew to New Orleans to announce the new franchise. The first owner was a young Houston oilman named John Mecom Jr. The team's colors reflected Louisiana's deep ties to the oil industry—and Mecom's. "Black gold," he explained. The name of the team was meant as a trumpet blast to the city's Catholic tradition and the most famous Dixieland song of all, "When the Saints Go Marching In."

All the team had to do now was play some football. That turned out to be the hard part.

Over the years, Saints fans had a few things to cheer about besides John Gilliam's first-day return. A few. Tom Dempsey, with half a foot, kicked a sixty-three-yard field goal in the final seconds of a 1970 game to beat the Detroit Lions, 19-17. That record was matched but never beaten.

After the 1992 season, the Saints sent four linebackers—Rickey Jackson, Vaughn Johnson, Sam Mills and Pat Swilling, "the Dome Patrol"—to the Pro Bowl. That was impressive. The Saints won their first play-off game in 2000, when St. Louis Rams receiver Az-Zahir Hakim dropped a punt with less than two minutes remaining to seal the 31-28 win.

"Hakim drops the ball! Hakim drops the ball," a hyperventilating Jim Henderson shouted on WWL Radio, a call Saints fans still love to imitate.

Archie Manning had a great passing arm and nimble dancing feet. Too bad he played on such lousy 1970s teams.

Coach Jim Mora, hired after Tom Benson bought the team in 1985, got some real traction in the late 1980s and early 1990s with quarterback Bobby Hebert. Unfortunately, Joe Montana, Jerry Rice and the San Francisco 49ers were also in the NFC West.

A New Orleans Saints All-Time Highlights Reel can be maddeningly short.

Early draft picks disappointed. First-round kicker Russell Erxleben. Running back Vaughn Dunbar and his incurable fumble-itis. And there was Ricky Williams, who made some contributions but cost the team eight draft picks, including two first-rounders. He and Coach Mike Ditka posed for *Sports Illustrated* in a wedding dress and a tuxedo. Ricky wore the dress.

Coaches came and went. Hank Stram. Bum Phillips. Bum's son, Wade. Ditka. Jim Haslett. Some had successful careers other places. Mora was the only one who won more Saints games than he lost.

There are a hundred ways to count all this. None of them is good. The Saints didn't climb as high as second in their division until 1979. They had only two .500 finishes in their first twenty years.

Every season started with promise. Most ended in sorrow, one more link in the chain of Saints disappointment.

The real low point came in 1980, when the Saints lost fourteen games in a row. Sportscaster Buddy Diliberto urged fans to wear paper bags on their heads. Many took a certain perverse pleasure at each new embarrassment committed by "the 'Aints."

By 1985, Mecom had grown weary of football ownership and was ready to sell the Saints. The likely new owner? An investor group prepared to move the team to Jacksonville,

Florida. This would have meant the end of the New Orleans Saints. As that deal got closer, there was talk around New Orleans that Governor Edwin Edwards was putting together a group of local businesspeople who would buy the team and keep it here. When Tom Benson, who had built a successful chain of auto dealerships in the New Orleans area, was invited to a sit-down at the governor's office, he assumed he'd be meeting with the other members of the local investor group. Only after he arrived did he discover that there were no other investors. He was the group.

Mr. Benson had never owned a professional sports franchise. He'd never been a major Saints fan. He just wanted to see the team stay in New Orleans, and he agreed to go it alone. He paid $78 million. He hired Jim Finks as the team's general manager. Finks became his mentor in the football business, and the fortunes of the team brightened noticeably.

But still.

It was one thing for the Saints to go 3-11 in their inaugural season. They were, after all, an expansion team. But a 3-13 record thirty-eight years later in the Katrina year of 2005 and only one play-off victory in between? There was still some work to be done.

In my last visit with Bill Parcells before I came to New Orleans, he, like Jerry Jones, gave me some insightful advice. "You've got to figure out what's kept that organization from winning," Bill said to me. "Quickly. Figure it out quickly. Or three years from now, they'll be having another press conference announcing the hiring of another new coach."

Parcells went on to talk about our league and new coaches. There were ten that year in 2006, ten out of thirty-two teams. That's almost a third of the league.

"Of those ten," he said, "only one or two of you will have some success. The others will fail. Those are just the statistics if you research new hires."

That was not an encouraging number. But Parcells had it right. Penguins were what popped into my mind. Have you ever seen one of those documentaries about penguins jumping off an iceberg to get to another iceberg? Ten jump into the water. Only a couple make it across. The rest get eaten. And yet the penguins still jump, even knowing the odds.

I understood Bill's point. "These jobs were open for a reason," he said. Despite all the optimism of the new hires, the original problems never got corrected. The problems just ate someone new.

Whatever the dysfunction might be—and I really didn't know yet—it had to be repaired top to bottom, across the organization. How we traveled. How we ate. How we sold tickets. And, yes, how we played football. We had to look at everything. We had to look at everything under a microscope. We had to find the right quarterback and the right guys working in the locker room. And we needed a whole organization to support what we were doing.

It's very easy to put all the prior failures on the old coaching staff and the old team. They are gone. But they are not the whole story.

Mr. Benson seemed to understand this and asked if I would address the whole organization after he introduced me as the new head coach.

"We'll win as an organization," I said that day in the building cafeteria, "not just a team."

8

NEW HOME

MONDAY MORNING, I FLEW in from Dallas on Mr. Benson's plane. It was Gary Gibbs and me. Gary, who had been with me in Dallas, was a very talented coach and a good friend, and he'd agreed to come to New Orleans as our defensive coordinator. Mickey had arranged for us to stay at an old Wyndham the team had used before Katrina. That hotel gave me an early hint of what we might be up against.

There was a horrible, musty smell in the room. I'd brought three garment bags with me. I knew I wouldn't be back in Dallas for another couple months. When I opened the closet and hung up the garment bags, the rod snapped immediately, dumping all three bags onto the nasty carpet that covered the floor.

I opened the TV cabinet and the door fell off in my hand. The whole hotel was like a sitcom. I was beginning to realize that even the places that were open here were not quite ready for business.

When I mentioned this to the people at the front desk, nobody seemed especially surprised. Truly, it was every little thing. Gary requested a wake-up call for six the next morning. The call didn't come. "Ma'am," he said later to the lady at the front desk, "I put in for a wake-up call this morning, and it never came."

The woman nodded. "Well," she said with a shrug, "sometimes it works. Sometimes it doesn't. Been that way since the storm."

Gary and I looked at each other. Then Gary said, "Well, if sometimes it doesn't work, then it's not a wake-up call."

You couldn't minimize the storm. It had a profound impact on the whole region. Its effects are still being felt. You couldn't live in that time and place and not understand this. But still, I thought, if we're going to make real progress—if the city and region are—we can't start giving in to Katrina despair.

Right there, one of the first things we agreed on, Gary and I, was that we would never blame the hurricane for any failure we might have. Even if it was responsible, we wouldn't blame it. That became an inside joke with us and with the other coaches as they began to arrive. Whenever something didn't go right, whatever it was, we'd roll our eyes and say: "Katrina?"

By the second day at Hotel Hell, Gary and I had run out of patience with that dump. "All right," I told Gary, "we're not gonna be in this hotel long." When we got to the office, I went in to see Mickey immediately.

"If we want any chance of hiring any coaches or signing any players," I said, "the last place we want to put them is in that hotel." He laughed and agreed, and we moved to the Airport Hilton. That was one of the few places that had hunkered down and stayed open during the whole mess of Katrina. They could handle a wake-up call. They had a housekeeping staff. They had a restaurant, even if the menu was somewhat limited. I can still recite to you verbatim every item they had. We ate there almost every night. Most important, they had a general manager named Craig Mooney who understood the idea of service, even at a difficult time. He was a great role model for a city pulling itself back up. He never blamed anything on Katrina. That hotel was our home for seven months while we began to build a football team.

Every day, I would go into the office on Airline Drive. I say *the* office, not *my* office. My office wasn't ready yet. Lots of things around the office weren't ready yet. The Saints staff was still getting settled back in New Orleans after San Antonio. They were still having trouble finding painters and carpenters. But we had to get started, nice accommodations or not. And we did.

Mickey and I would sit there with two depth charts on the wall of my makeshift work space, going through the personnel. One chart was coaches. The other was players. Who was already here? Who did we have a chance of getting? What were our biggest needs? The needs were so great, it was hard to know even where to begin.

Priority number one: hiring a coaching staff. I would need sixteen, seventeen, maybe eighteen assistant coaches. That's what it takes to run an NFL team. I had to find them, hire them, convince them to come and get them on board.

The Senior Bowl is held in Mobile every January. It's a two-hour drive from New Orleans, and it's also a place to hire coaches. I was interviewing a defensive line coach by the name of Bill Kollar. He flew into New Orleans. We interviewed at the Saints complex, and he traveled with me to Mobile. The drive from New Orleans to Mobile after Katrina, if you hadn't seen it already, might have been the worst two-hour stretch of highway on Earth. For a good year after Katrina, it was like that.

There were boats on the side of the road. Casinos that had moved and tumbled. Just unthinkable devastation all along this road. At one point Bill said, "You know, you're lucky my kids are out of the house or you'd have no chance of hiring me." Two days later he took the same job with the Buffalo Bills.

I tried to get permission to hire Tony Sparano from the Dallas Cowboys. He was under contract. That permission was denied by Parcells. I tried to hire Dave Magazu of the Carolina Panthers. Permission denied. Aaron Kromer, Tampa Bay Buccaneers. Permission denied. These were guys I knew well and had worked with.

I got a call about Pete Carmichael. Pete was a quality-control coach at San Diego. He agreed to come. Now he was going to be my quarterbacks coach. Pete looks just like the Dustin Hoffman character in the movie *Papillon*. He has the wire-rimmed glasses and same kind of smile. He was a really good baseball player at Boston College but doesn't look athletic at all. He's very intelligent and sharp on the computer, and he has a great work ethic. Pete was the third or fourth coach I was able to hire.

One thing we figured out in a hurry: There weren't a lot of experienced NFL coaches just itching to come to New Orleans. It would take a special coach to want this job. Or someone who would come for a special opportunity like a chance to move from college to the pros or for a promotion in the NFL.

Our strength coach, Dan Dalrymple, we hired from Miami University in Oxford, Ohio. It was his first NFL job. Curtis Johnson, New Orleans native and receivers coach, came from the University of Miami for his first NFL job. Gary Gibbs, who came with me from Dallas, was now defensive coordinator, his first coordinator's job. The line coach, Marion Hobby, I hired out of Clemson. Terry Malone, the tight ends coach, came from college too, the University of Michigan. Greg McMahon came out of East Carolina University to be assistant to special teams. Doug Marrone I had to pry out of the New York Jets, where he was an offensive line coach and would be our offensive coordinator, a nice step up.

It's not that these guys weren't talented or driven or great. But they'd all come for a significant promotion or the opportunity to work in the NFL. They and their families were taking the same risk all of us were.

Joe Vitt was the big exception. You remember the movie *Cool Hand Luke?* Not the Paul Newman character—Luke's buddy, Dragline. That big, blond-haired prisoner who was talking all the time. George Kennedy played him. Won the Academy Award. The prisoners would gather around his bunk, and he'd tell stories. That's Joe Vitt. Not from a stature point of view. Joe just has a way of making you laugh. He'd been in the NFL for twenty-seven years when he came to New Orleans. Like George Kennedy on his bunk bed, Joe would tell these stories, and all of us would listen—maybe a story about Chuck Knox, or he'd give you the history of the league in the seventies. I gave him the title of assistant head coach. Ninety percent of the time in the NFL, that just means more money or a title to keep someone happy. But if you went to the dictionary and looked up "NFL assistant head coach," you'd see a picture of Joe Vitt. He's from South Jersey—very, very much to the point. He can handle a lot of headaches. He was going to be a great ally to me as a first-year head coach. He was behind many of the motivational ideas that were credited to me. He was my consigliere—that's exactly what he was. Vitt had finished the 2005 season as head coach of the St. Louis Rams after Mike Martz took ill. Joe wasn't keeping the Rams job permanently, but he had five other offers on the table. He was one of the most respected linebacker coaches in the league. And he was just crazy enough to come. Both his children were grown, freeing him from the concerns that some younger coaches had. He had a beach house in Ocean City, Maryland, and his wife could tell him where to mail the checks. Other than the signing of Drew Brees, this was the most important acquisition we made.

As they trickled in, all these coaches were in New Orleans without their families. Every now and then, somebody's wife—or wife and kids—would come to visit. It was always a little strained. I got a special visit from Beth, Meghan and Connor on Valentine's Day weekend, our first family get-together in New Orleans.

At this point, Beth was just taking a peek to check out the area, getting a feel for things in this crazy place that was going to be our home.

I was in a pinch. My wife was coming. It was Valentine's Day. I knew I needed something strong. So I went to the local jeweler, Aucoin Hart on Metairie Road. They're a terrific jeweler. We still have a fine relationship with them. I got her some glittery, expensive diamond necklace. I would have been much better off with something simple. It just reeked of a last-minute buy.

"I got this for you," I said, handing her the box soon after she and the kids arrived at the Airport Hilton.

She opened it slowly, and she didn't say anything at first.

But I could see a pained look spreading across her face. Beth is an understanding woman and a supportive wife. God knows I've tested this over the years. But she could tell the necklace wasn't thought out.

"No," Beth said. "No. Definitely not." She handed the box back to me.

The necklace was a tremendous failure. She wouldn't take it. It was just awful. It might as well have been ten thousand dollars in cash in a brown paper bag. It was the antithesis of what I was shooting for. I told her I'd return it on Monday.

That was how the whole visit went. Like quicksand. Every time I wiggled, I'd sink farther down. We were hanging on here, and I mean that. It was tough.

And the kids weren't exactly having a blast. Meghan had strep throat. I asked our medical staff to call in a prescription for antibiotics to CVS. The store on Airline Drive is about three miles from the Airport Hilton. Airline Drive isn't the place you'd want your family to get their impression of New Orleans. It's the old highway to Baton Rouge. There's nothing appealing about it at all. There are really only two or three decent buildings on that part of the road besides the Saints facility: Cox Cable, the local Budweiser headquarters, St. Martin's School.

I left the hotel about six p.m. to pick up Meghan's medication. It's about a ten-minute drive. I got to the drugstore.

There was a line. About forty-five minutes later, Beth was on the cell phone.

"What are you doing?" she asked.

"I'm in line," I said.

One person behind the counter was trying to fill prescriptions. I don't know what the problem was. But I was getting impatient. This was just a couple of months after my hiring. I could stand in a line or be anywhere publicly and not be recognized. The line was hardly moving at all.

My wife called a second time. "What's taking so long?" And a third time. "Sean, you're kidding me." Beth called a total of four times.

When I finally got to the counter, the woman could give me only half the prescription. They're out of it. They're limited. They're rationing. I don't know what the problem was. All I knew was I was at the CVS. Beth was at the hotel with our sick child. The necklace was in its box to go back to the jeweler. We were in a city where the pharmacies didn't function. And I'd been told no by four or five different coaches in the last couple weeks. I stood in line for that amoxicillin for two hours and ten minutes.

"Sean, where are you bringing us?" Beth asked when I finally got back to the hotel.

9

SETTLING IN

WE HAD TO PUT a calendar together for the team. It was the first calendar I'd ever done. You have to lay it all out. I thought about what Parcells did when he came to Dallas. When's your first team meeting? When does your off-season program begin? What does the league schedule say?

All of this gets filed with the league office back in New York.

Periodically, players would come into the office. Some players weren't in town, but we spoke to everybody. We told ourselves, "We're gonna look at them all as equals. We're gonna play the best players. We're gonna go by what we see." We knew we had to make some decisions in regard to free agency. We were going to lose our starting center, LeCharles Bentley. We were moving on from Aaron Brooks, the quarterback: "Call him and tell him we're gonna waive him." There were others we would have to waive as well.

There was a divide in the building that was important to understand. When a coaching staff gets fired, the coach and his assistants all go away. But the marketing guy, the tickets guy, the PR guy—these people remain. They've seen lots of coaches come and go. There's always a load of blame that goes out the door.

To his credit, Mr. Benson knew there was a cavity that needed to be filled, an unhealthy vibe, a bridge that needed to be built. He had mentioned this in my initial interview. And the problem was caused by both sides, not just one. So in the same way we were evaluating the players, we were evaluating everyone—from who's cooking the meals on up. A to Z, we were evaluating. Do they have the passion? Are they just punching the clock? Everyone came under scrutiny.

Two months into the job, our coaching staff was pretty much complete. We were in a personnel meeting when one of the Saints executives poked his head into the room. "Coach, I just want to bring you some information on the car program here," he said. "I'm gonna hand this packet to your coaches."

I looked and didn't say anything.

He went through the mileage restrictions, the return policy and about a hundred other rules and regulations. At some point, I stopped listening to him. It just rubbed me the wrong way. He finished and left. I closed the door and looked around the room. "Pay no attention to what he just said," I told the coaches. I went down to see Mickey right away.

"This is not a time for a lot of stupid technicalities," I said. "If a guy wants to live on the Northshore, he shouldn't have to worry about how many miles he's putting on his car. We need to look closely at the company policy on relocation.

If a coach has to be in the hotel for more than two months—well, these aren't normal circumstances. Can you please tell our car guy, no more surprise visits?"

We had our first full team meeting on March 15. We were going to address our off-season conditioning program. It was one of the most important meetings we were going to have, my first team meeting ever as a head coach. Before the meeting, the players were gathering in the locker room. I'll never forget walking into that meeting and introducing the coaches. I felt like I was standing in front of the Sweathogs from *Welcome Back, Kotter*. Guys slouched in their chairs, looking off in all directions, making comments under their breath. The demeanor of the team was just awful. Revealing too. There was a left tackle named Wayne Gandy. Wayne was one of the leaders in the offensive line, thirty-five years old, in the late stages of his career. And he had a La-Z-Boy recliner near his locker. Pretty soon, I was asking Dan Simmons—our head equipment manager who everyone calls Chief and has been in the organization the longest, longer than Mr. Benson or anybody else—"Whose is that?"

"It's Wayne Gandy's," Chief said.

"Do me a favor," I told him. "Can we have that removed, and just let Wayne know he can pick it up out on the loading dock?"

And the chair was gone.

I was going to address everything that could have anything to do with us winning or losing, and that included more than the offensive playbook and our red-zone defense. We'd already established that Katrina was not going to be a reason that we failed. Neither was lack of discipline. That was an important lesson I took from Parcells: You have to establish law and order right from the start. So we began in the locker room.

That was a couple days before St. Patrick's Day. New Orleans is a very Catholic city. St. Patrick's Day is a big deal. And we had several Irish-Catholics on the first-year coaching staff, besides me. We figured this was as good a time as any to go out and blow off some steam.

That first year, besides his football duties, special teams coordinator John Bonamego was also our food and beverage director. John put together a St. Patrick's itinerary for us.

St. Patty's Day fell on a Friday. We finished work and a limo bus picked everyone up at the Hilton. We had dinner at Chartres House Café and then walked over to Pat O'Brien's for some hurricanes and cigars. We were definitely ready.

Need more proof New Orleans was still struggling? It was St. Patrick's Day, and Pat O'Brien's was only one-third full. The city was just barely getting off the mat. We're in Pat O's, for Christ's sake! In the piano bar with the dueling piano players! It's St. Patty's Day! And we had no trouble finding seats, sixteen of them together! We had a long table right by one of the pianos. The coaches were dropping bills in an otherwise empty tip jar. They were calling out requests for "American Pie" and their college fight songs. Nobody had any idea who these obnoxious people were.

Part of the oddness of the room might have been because Eddie Gabriel was gone. When I visited the bar on my occasional trips to New Orleans, I was totally charmed by Eddie. They called him the Rhythm King. He was one of those never-miss-a-day-of-work kind of guys. Eddie had been at Pat O'Brien's sixty-seven years. With a tray of coins, a set of thimbles on his fingers and an infectious personality, he could keep up with both piano players and delight the whole room.

I asked about Eddie, of course. Charlie Bateman, the manager, told me the sad tale. Eddie left work the afternoon before Katrina. His wife was coming to get him, he said. He'd be fine. His body showed up four months later in a temporary morgue in St. Gabriel, Louisiana. He was among those who had drowned in the flood. His absence made the empty room seem even emptier.

We carried on as Eddie always had. We talked and laughed and shook our heads. Joe Vitt was telling stories about the Seattle Seahawks, what Chuck Knox was really like in 1981. We caught everyone up on our families back home. We talked about this great adventure we were embarking on, even if it was a total question mark. We pretended not to miss the creature comforts we were missing.

What a sight this crew was.

A couple of the guys had on Irish Guinness caps. Terry Malone was wearing a leprechaun hat. George Henshaw was standing on a chair singing "Rocky Top" and demanding to hear the West Virginia fight song. Big Dan Dalrymple was complaining that the rubber band on his hat had just broken. What did he expect? His hat size is $7\frac{7}{8}$. Somebody else's head was down on the table. Dennis Allen, who had hoped to go to Tampa, had finally gotten over being hired by us. He had his little St. Patty's Day hat on and wanted to hear the Aggie fight song from Texas A&M. A couple of the other guys were wearing Mardi Gras beads. Greg McMahon wanted to know where he could get a cigar rolled in the neighborhood. He took off around the corner and eventually missed the bus back to the hotel. He was our penguin who never made it to the next iceberg. He walked and then he got a ride and then he went to a police station and somehow eventually made it back to the hotel. But the beers kept coming. So did the hurricanes. And the night went late.

At one point, I looked over at Joe Vitt. He didn't crack a smile. Completely deadpan, he announced in a strong baritone: "After a long and exhaustive search, the New Orleans Saints have settled on their coaching staff."

10

GETTING DREW

WE HAD A WHIRLWIND twenty-four hours planned for Drew and Brittany Brees.

Finding the right quarterback, Mickey and I knew, would define the next chapter in the history of the Saints. Oh, and our careers might also be at stake.

Parcells used to say: "It's not like you can dial 1-800-GET-A-QUARTERBACK." Some teams had been dialing that number for ten or fifteen years, and still nobody answered. Drew was the most promising idea Mickey and I had come up with. Now we had to get him on the line.

In our short time together, this quick get-to-know-you visit, I wanted to get a personal feel for the injured San Diego quarterback. I wanted him to get a feel for us. So we toured the facility on Airline Drive. We sent Brittany to see the antiques stores and the funky shops on Magazine Street. After lunch I volunteered to drive our guests around to look at houses. I wanted Drew and especially Brittany to see that New Orleans wasn't a total disaster zone. There were places they might actually like to live.

I headed straight to the Northshore. That's where Beth and I had bought a spec home from a builder. It's an upscale suburban area across Lake Pontchartrain on the far side of the twenty-four-mile Causeway Bridge. Some people find the drive mind-numbing, but I didn't really mind it. In hindsight, the Northshore was probably not the place for Drew and Brittany. Uptown was more their style. But I remembered how Beth reacted the day our Realtor first drove her across the lake. "That's easy," she informed me. "I know where we're living." I was thinking the Northshore would seem safe and nonthreatening to a couple of out-of-towners arriving so soon after the storm.

I drove Drew and Brittany across the causeway. We pulled into a subdivision and a couple of gated communities. I showed them our half-completed house. Then we turned around and drove back over the bridge. And I got horribly lost.

Somehow I got off at the wrong exit. I was on I-10 in the right direction. I just made a wrong turn. I didn't exit at Clearview like I was supposed to. I ended up on a road that goes parallel to I-10, which made no sense at all. In my defense, I hadn't been in New Orleans very long by then. I didn't know all the roads. I had to call Mickey for directions. He was trying to figure out where we were. I thought I was running north-south, but I was driving farther west. The whole thing was becoming embarrassing.

I looked in the rearview mirror. Brittany was dozing in the backseat. Everyone was getting tired. This wasn't exactly the impression I was hoping to make.

"Listen," I finally admitted to Drew. "I have no idea where we are right now."

He just laughed.

I knew I was blowing the afternoon schedule. I thought to myself, "I might as well drive them to Miami right now."

But that winding drive did give me some extra one-on-one time with Drew. I talked about our plans for the offense. He told me about his rehab routine. We got some more hang-out time together. I didn't want him to leave saying, "I didn't have enough time with the head coach." He was certainly seeing one side of the head coach now, navigating incompetently across unfamiliar terrain. I hoped he wouldn't read too much into that: *This is who I'll be playing for?*

There was nothing more important to us than finding the right quarterback—and getting him here. At first, we thought we might find a good one in the college draft. We had the second pick that year, after the Houston Texans. That's the nice part of 3-13, the only nice part.

But the track record for new coaches drafting quarterbacks early—it isn't good at all. Chris Palmer with Tim Couch in Cleveland. Marty Mornhinweg with Joey Harrington in Detroit. It's been one disappointment after another. Once in a while, there's an Andy Reid drafting a Donovan McNabb. But given the history, you'd really have to love someone to take that chance. John Fox was faced with that choice when he became head coach of the Carolina Panthers. He passed on Harrington and grabbed defensive end Julius Peppers instead. He was immediately glad he did.

Over the years, there have also been some talented quarterbacks already in the building who the Saints had allowed to leave. Jake Delhomme went off to Carolina while the Saints stuck with Aaron Brooks. Marc Bulger went to St. Louis and was the Pro Bowl MVP in 2004. That said, we were on the quarterback hunt.

We'd begun by evaluating three college quarterbacks who might be available in the draft. Jay Cutler, who was coming out of Vanderbilt. Vince Young from Texas. Matt Leinart from Southern Cal. It was the end of February. But we hadn't gotten too far into that when word began to spread: Drew Brees was not re-signing with the San Diego Chargers.

After the 2005 season, the Chargers had offered Brees an incentive-based contract where most of the money was not guaranteed. He read the incentive-based offer as a sign of no confidence by the Chargers and demanded the type of money a top-five "franchise" quarterback would receive.

When the Chargers refused to budge, Brees began looking for another team. The New Orleans Saints and the Miami Dolphins expressed the most interest.

It's an amazing concept now: Drew Brees as a free agent in the winter of 2006. Bum-rushed out of San Diego. Told his quarterbacking services were not required. Dumped on the open market like some afterthought eBay item that might or might not generate a couple bids.

Actually, it was amazing even then.

Brees, who'd just turned twenty-seven, was an undeniable talent. He'd led Purdue to three bowl games, including the 2001 Rose Bowl. Some college commentators had wondered: At six foot one, was he too small to be a top-level quarterback in the pros? But he was drafted by San Diego at the start of the second round in 2001, and in three years he brought the Chargers into the play-offs. In 2002, he took over from Doug Flutie as starting quarterback. Although

Flutie jumped back into the starting role for part of 2003, Drew was leading the offense again in 2004. That year, he was named NFL Comeback Player of the Year. And it wasn't just what he was doing in the numbers. Everywhere he went, on and off the field, Drew Brees was known as a leader—the kind of quarterback who makes a whole offense want to play for him.

But there was a real issue. In the last game of 2005, he injured his throwing shoulder when he dove on a fumble in his own end zone and 325-pound Denver Broncos tackle Gerard Warren landed on him. Drew was flown to Birmingham, Alabama, for arthroscopic surgery. On January 6, Dr. James Andrews repaired a 360-degree tear of the labrum and a deep, partial tear of the rotator cuff. The renowned orthopedic surgeon called Drew's busted right shoulder "one of the most unique injuries of any athlete I've treated," telling *Sports Illustrated*: "Lord, I was just hoping to give him a functional shoulder. An average athlete would not recover from this."

But if the Chargers were not re-signing Brees, what possibilities did he offer the Saints? That's what Mickey and I were asking ourselves. If the injury was as scary as Dr. Andrews was saying, would the surgery work? What would the recovery be like? Did the Chargers know something we didn't? We had no doubts about Drew's native ability or the intensity of his work ethic. But how soon, if ever, would his precision and his strength be back?

We also knew we weren't the only team that was thinking about him. The Miami Dolphins were looking closely. And the early word in the NFL was that Drew, who'd loved the San Diego lifestyle, could happily see himself in the South

Florida sun. Didn't anyone ever warn this guy about the dangers of UV rays?

One thing we knew: We had to take some risk here. With so much stacked against us, the Saints could not afford to be a play-it-safe team. We were recruiting players other teams were overlooking. We'd put coaches in jobs they'd never done before. And Drew Brees, the more we thought about him, seemed like just the kind of quarterback we might want to take a chance on. This was as much a judgment of Drew's character and work ethic as of his abilities. Digging into his background, I could tell. He'd always been a winner. Physically gifted, hugely competitive, intensely focused. Good things just happened to him. Drew was the boy who knocked over three bottles at the carnival and won the big stuffed animal for the girl. In his two years as starting quarterback, his team at Austin's Westlake High had gone 28-0-1. He was an avid teenage tennis player, challenging and beating a young Andy Roddick. He had giant hands and could dunk a basketball. Success just followed him around.

Even though he had a risky shoulder, how could we not make a run at Brees?

I was excited. But I was guarded too. I knew better than to get ahead of myself. I knew the injury was an issue. I knew the Dolphins wanted him. I didn't want to feel the way I had at Miami University when Ohio State swooped in and grabbed a hot recruit.

We were lucky to have Pete Carmichael as our quarterbacks coach. Having worked with Drew in San Diego, Pete had some insights into Drew's way of thinking. And Drew had some comfort with Pete.

Other than our little traffic mishap, I felt like the visit went well. That evening, we had dinner at a back table at Emeril's. Emeril Lagasse, the restaurant's renowned chef, was in New York that night, but he left a gift for Drew. It was a copy of one of Emeril's cookbooks with a note inside: "If you come to New Orleans, I'll come to your new house and cook your first meal." Now there's a chef who knows how to make a newcomer feel welcome!

In speaking to Drew, Mickey and I took the same approach Mickey had taken with me. We were completely frank with Drew about the team and New Orleans. "Here are the problems. Here are the logistical issues. And here are the opportunities." And I think we put on an absolutely excellent show.

The offensive coaches—Pete, Johnny Morton, Doug Marrone—created a thoughtful PowerPoint presentation of our goals for the offense. They showed video cut-ups of Drew's own plays and then similar plays I'd run in Dallas and New York. We wanted Drew to feel like New Orleans was a place he'd fit in. We wanted him to feel like we really wanted him. We had to lay it all out because, honestly, we didn't have a track record to point at. I was a first-year head coach. We hadn't been at this for four or five years. We weren't able to say, "This is what we've done already. We'll keep doing it." All we had was our vision and ourselves. We were really selling ourselves. Joe Vitt, Pete Carmichael, Doug Marrone, Johnny Morton, Gary Gibbs, Mickey Loomis, Mr. Benson and me—everyone in the process struck a single, unequivocal note: We want you. We want you a lot.

But hovering over the whole situation, there was still a strong dynamic of uncertainty. How could there not be? There was uncertainty everywhere. The uncertainty of the Saints. The uncertainty of the city. And the uncertainty of

Drew's shoulder. What happens if another storm blows in? What happens if the shoulder blows out?

We were living with that uncertainty every day. Three weeks earlier, I was at the CVS, waiting in line. Six weeks earlier, Drew was on Dr. Andrews's table. He knew about uncertainty too. Maybe that would give us some kind of edge. Here's the thing we were certain about: We wanted him, and we were willing to take a chance.

I knew the Dolphins. If they were keen on Drew, they'd make a formidable case. They were going to be thorough. Drew was going to visit Miami right after he left us. Jason Garrett was coaching the quarterbacks there. I knew he and his wife, Brill, would give a great Miami tour. There was a lot more stability with that team and that city than we could offer. But in the end, the Dolphins were less decisive than we were, and that made all the difference in the world.

It turned out that the doctors in Miami had some qualms. Maybe they lacked the faith that we had—or the willingness to take a chance. For whatever combination of reasons, their doctors ultimately gave Drew a lower recovery score than ours did. The contract they were willing to offer him reflected that. Frankly, it wasn't in the same ballpark as ours. They bet against the shoulder. We bet for the man.

I knew the two of us, working together, could complete each other—and create greatness.

My understanding. His skill.

When we were putting together our contract proposal for Drew, Mickey asked me the same two questions he likes to ask when we are weighing a potential hire: "Coach, do you want him?" And if the answer is yes, "Where do we have to be with our offer to separate ourselves from anyone else?"

Because of all the uncertainty that we came with, we knew we had to be an extra step, maybe two extra steps, above the competition. Working with Drew's agent, Tom Condon, Mickey proposed a long-term deal that would make Drew the Saints' franchise quarterback and in many ways the public face of the team. I give Mickey a ton of credit for his ability to craft a contract that would work well for both sides. I like to joke: "My job is to set the table. His job is to pay for the meal." Our offer included $10 million in guaranteed money the first year and a $12 million option the second year.

There was a boldness to our offer. When you take that approach, you risk someone saying later, "Boy, the Saints overpaid there." It could happen. Sometimes, it has. But when you're in the position we were in at the start of 2006, taking a chance is part of the equation. A chance is what we took.

Several days after Drew's Miami visit, I got the call. He was signing a six-year, $60 million deal with the Saints. I was thrilled. At that point, we celebrated every little step forward, and this was a big one. The victories didn't come so easily back then. I felt like I had won when I hired Joe Vitt. This was something special. This was something we could build on. There were plenty of roadblocks yet to come. There were lots of things that still weren't going the way they should. I still had that team official nagging me about the car program. But, one by one, we learned to handle those challenges. We celebrated each victory and moved on.

11

GETTING REGGIE

REGGIE BUSH WAS DEVASTATED.

It was the night before the 2006 NFL Draft, and word was leaking out. The Houston Texans, who had the first pick, were taking the big defensive end Mario Williams from NC State. It wasn't a crazy choice on Houston's part. World-class defensive ends—they don't show up often—cause turnovers and win football games.

But to Reggie Bush, this was a dis of major proportions.

Reggie was the best college running back in America. He'd won the Heisman Trophy. He was versatile and strong. He could carry, catch and return both punts and kicks—a genuine triple threat. He'd been a key part of two national championship teams at the University of Southern California. He was *supposed* to go first in the draft. It wasn't just that Reggie had his heart set on Houston or even the nice ego rush of being number one. Reggie and his team of advisers were fully aware of which team had the second pick.

We did.

Reggie was at a hotel in New York City. His agent, Joel Segal, was there. So was his marketing agent, Mike Ornstein. Reggie's whole entourage was there. And not one of them sounded the least bit pleased. Mickey and I were in Mickey's office. We took a call from New York.

Now, I'd never met Mike Ornstein before. I'd seen him around Dallas with Parcells. I just knew he did some stuff with Reebok, and he was handling Reggie's marketing. I started with no presumptions about him either way.

Ornstein got right to the point.

"Gentlemen," he said, "look. The Texans are gonna take Mario. Reggie does not want to play in New Orleans. He wants to be in a bigger market. This is not who you want to draft. You need to understand: This kid doesn't want to come there."

Ornstein had some crazy idea about a trade we might cobble together with the Jets and some other team. Somehow, he said, we'd be better off that way. He assured us we didn't want a player who didn't want to play for us.

I glanced at Mickey. I knew he was thinking the same thing I was. I leaned closer to the speakerphone.

"Fuck you," I said and hung up the phone.

Now, we were as surprised as anyone that we had a genuine crack at Reggie Bush. In all our predraft scenarios, that possibility had not been discussed much.

The weekend before the draft, Kenny Chesney was playing at the Cajundome in Lafayette. Beth and I, and Mickey and his fiancée, Melanie, drove out to see him. We talked draft possibilities there and back. Not a word about Reggie. On Wednesday, we drove to the Lower Ninth Ward for a Habitat for Humanity project. President Bush was there that day. "Who are you selecting?" he wanted to know. I told him we figured Houston was taking Reggie, and we still weren't sure. Friday night, as the draft was getting started at Radio City Music Hall in New York, five of us went to dinner at Emeril's.

That's become an annual tradition for us before each college draft. Rick Reiprish, Rick Mueller, Russ Ball, Mickey and me—the college director, the pro director, the cap guy, the GM and the head coach. We weigh the players we're looking at. We obsess over every imaginable choice. We line up our contingencies. But, really, the work has been done. The hay is in the barn.

As I sat down at the restaurant table, I knew something the others did not. Their BlackBerrys hadn't lit up yet. Just before I'd come in, I'd gotten an early heads-up from a reliable NFL insider about Houston's real intentions that night.

"Hey," I said, as I pulled up my chair. "Texans aren't takin' Bush."

"Aw, you're nuts." "You're crazy." "You don't know what you're talking about."

"I'm telling you, they're not taking Bush," I said.

The other four were all so sure of themselves, someone proposed a bet. Twenty dollars a man. I'd be out eighty dollars if Reggie went to Houston.

I knew this was the easiest eighty dollars I would ever make. I knew that, at that exact moment, Houston was in contract discussions with the Williams camp. But no one believed me until I got up to use the restroom and, I guess, the BlackBerrys began to buzz. I got back to the table. Sitting next to my water glass were four twenty-dollar bills.

That would cover my blackened redfish and wine.

We finished dinner and drove back to the Saints complex on Airline Drive. We were almost giddy from the possibility of Reggie as a Saint. Or was it that nice bottle of Caymus? Either way, we began to get our heads around the prospect of drafting Reggie Bush. What a great addition to the backfield! Reggie and popular Saints running back Deuce McAllister, a backfield one-two punch! Love him on special teams! And how excited the fans would be!

We parked our cars and headed up to Mickey's office. We had our speakerphone call with Ornstein, our New York friend. A few minutes later, Mr. Benson came in. With the owner were his granddaughter, Rita Benson LeBlanc, and his grandson, Ryan LeBlanc. They were eager to analyze all the possibilities. There was some discussion of whether we should trade away the Reggie pick.

I remember saying very calmly, "If we don't select this guy as the second pick of the draft, it'll be the worst thing we've ever done as an organization." By the end of the night, everyone was on board.

We had a huge tailgate party the next day in an open field near the facility on Airline Drive. Draft Day Fan Fest was sponsored by WWL Radio, the flagship station broadcasting Saints games, and the public was invited to come. There was a live band and free food. These were the hard-core Saints fans, a widely diverse mix of black and white, young and old, rich and poor and in between, a great cross-section of the region. In some cities the core NFL fan is a corporate suit with a hefty expense account. In New Orleans it's some of them and a whole lot of families who come out for the beer and the food.

"We're getting Reggie," they kept telling each other excitedly.

"Can you believe it? We're getting Reggie."

I'd met many Saints fans since I'd come to New Orleans, but mostly in ones and small groups. They were everything I'd been told they'd be, even in these post-Katrina days. Warm. Friendly. Completely without pretense. Utterly loyal to their team. They certainly hadn't gotten much encouragement over the years, not in the form of victories anyway. But this was my first experience seeing them in a larger number. What energy and enthusiasm they had! These were the people, year after year, who'd chosen to believe when Saints officials said: "Wait till next year"—and then after another disappointing season, chose to believe again: "Wait till next year."

This was the "Who Dat Nation" I'd been hearing about.

"Who dat?" they chanted.

"Who dat? Who dat say dey gonna beat dem Saints? Who dat?"

Were we finally going to give them something to cheer about?

Their exuberance, their patience and their love for one another were impossible not to feel. You could not meet these people—stand around and talk with them—without marveling for at least a moment how full of life they were, even this soon after Katrina.

"We pulled a fast one on the Texans," one man told me, quite conspiratorially.

When I protested that the Texans were skipping Reggie all on their own, he smiled at me and winked. "Don't worry," he said. "It'll be our little secret."

These are the kinds of people I like to conspire with! Finally, they were getting a Saints draft worth their excitement.

Between the first and second picks, the Jets did call. But the offer they were dangling wasn't remotely enough. Within a minute of his saying "No, thank you" to the Jets, our selection was made. And when word reached Fan Fest, the band stopped playing and people began to cheer.

Whether he wanted to or not, Reggie was coming to New Orleans!

Acting on his own, Drew called Reggie that afternoon. Coming from San Diego, Reggie knew exactly who Drew was, and this call was critical. It was classic Drew Brees. He was a real team leader before he'd ever put on a Saints uniform. The call helped ease Reggie's disappointment about New Orleans.

The PGA Tour happened to be in town that same weekend. It was one of the first big events that had come to New Orleans after the storm. So the city was crowded for a change. Reggie and his agents flew in on a private jet. We were taking them to dinner back at Emeril's. I know it sounds like we went to Emeril's a lot. But you have to understand it was one of the only restaurants at that time we knew would be crowded. Lots of places weren't open yet. Because of the golf weekend, the restaurant was especially packed.

On the limo ride from Airline Drive to the restaurant, I remember thinking to myself: This was the antithesis of what Parcells would do with a first-round pick. "Never fly your first-round pick in early," he once said. "Never drive him around in a limo. And never, ever put him in the presidential suite at the five-star Loews."

We walked into the restaurant—Mickey, Reggie, the two

agents and me. The crowd recognized Reggie immediately. All of a sudden, people in the restaurant were chanting: "Reggie! Reggie! Reggie!"

It was an amazing moment. It reminded me of the Muhammad Ali chants in the week leading up to the Joe Frazier fight. I was really quite moved. So was Reggie. Even Mike Ornstein had a beaming look on his face. Nobody was saying "Fuck you" anymore. The scene in the restaurant was so perfect, it almost seemed planned.

Shortly after we were seated, a woman came over and handed her daughter's cell phone number to Reggie's agent. "Would you give this to him?" she asked.

"You set this up?" Reggie asked me.

I had to tell him: "Really? You think the last twenty-four hours were spent staging your arrival? We had a draft to worry about."

And I wanted to make something clear: "This is the last limo ride," I told him. "The last fancy dinner, the last presidential suite. Save your shampoo from the Loews. We have to play some football. You're at the Airport Hilton next week."

Mike Ornstein loved hearing that. This was his language. He understood the rude awakening that awaited college stars as they entered the NFL. He'd seen it before.

And Reggie's arrival turned out to be a real shot in the arm for the whole franchise, whatever hesitation there might have been at first. Brees was here. Now Reggie too. It brought excitement. It would soon bring ticket sales. There would be tangible, financial benefits. The city was a third smaller than it had been before the storm, and for the first time in Saints history, season tickets would sell out.

That was saying something at a time like this.

I could see the growing excitement over Drew and Reggie—and feel it—everywhere I went. People saying, "Thank you." People saying, "It's looking good." People saying, "I know we've said this before, Coach, but this could be the year."

One night, Beth and I were at a concert at the New Orleans Arena. We were waiting in the beer line when a gentleman came up to me and said, "I'm not back at work yet. But I just went and got four season tickets—two for my brother and his wife, two for my wife and me. I'm out of a job, but I'm not worried. We can't wait to see your team play."

Now, what would make someone who wasn't working spend a couple of thousand dollars for a package of football tickets? It had to be more than a love for football. It was a sense that the team was coming back. There was real momentum. And this was the most important part: Supporting this team was a way of supporting this city. That's how intertwined they were.

I felt so grateful to that man and to thousands of others like him. This was early in the suffering for so many people. They were deep in recovery. Huge sacrifices were taking place. You knew the money for these season tickets didn't come easily. You can't take that lightly when you look at how someone chooses to spend entertainment dollars.

There are not many teams in any sport that can point to such a spike in support. And it came at an impossible time for the region.

It started with Drew Brees and Reggie Bush.

In the time since then, Mike Ornstein and I have become good friends. He has represented me in some of my business dealings. I've come to understand that he is not someone easily offended by casual language. Actually, those words are like "Good morning" to Mike. Just a regular conversation. No big deal. He told me later that he had passed along my speakerphone message to Reggie, softening it only a bit.

"These guys are gonna draft you," he told his client. "Get over it."

To his credit, despite whatever misgivings he might have had about New Orleans, Reggie was gracious from the start. I tried to be mindful, of course, about what had gone on, what was said in New York. Reggie was just twenty-one. He was a junior coming out of college. Those players at the top of the draft—they're pulled in so many directions. I'm sure he felt disappointment at the uncertainty of New Orleans and playing for a first-year coach. Same as I felt disappointment about not going to Green Bay and Drew felt disappointment about missing the Miami sun.

All of us had reservations, and all of us were here.

There was some lingering concern about how Reggie and Deuce McAllister would complement each other, concern on both their parts, I think. I sat down with Deuce and told him Reggie's arrival wasn't going to impact his role negatively. I said, "Let me as the head coach figure out how to use you guys in a plan. Trust me. There will be plenty of snaps for both of you, plenty of offense for both backs—both uniquely different."

Both the new guys, Reggie and Drew, immediately embedded themselves in the community. Even before they came to practice, they made themselves impossible not to like. They helped raise money for rebuilding groups. They turned up at media events. Both set up their own charitable foundations. And the team was gaining momentum too.

That first draft was very successful for us. It produced Roman Harper, Marques Colston, Jahri Evans—several key starters on our Super Bowl team.

More important, it showed me that my early intuition about our general manager, Mickey Loomis, was turning out to be right. He was exactly who I'd thought he was when I first interviewed with him. He was calm and organized and a good decision maker. He had none of the ego that is so prevalent in our league. He had a unique way of moving all parties to a good decision without grabbing credit. He was the quiet man in the corner who is somehow behind every good idea. He was just as excited as I was about Reggie and Drew.

In the next four years, this Payton-Loomis relationship was going to flourish.

12

GETTING READY

THE NFL HAS STRICT rules about how and when a team can practice in the off-season. There are calendars and dates, and even some special exceptions for a team that has a new head coach. From the moment we went to work in New Orleans, our attitude was "We have so much to do here. Let's get started now." We knew we'd be making extraordinary demands on the players. We knew—and they discovered quickly—that they had never worked so hard in their lives. We all knew that crafting this team into winners would be very, very difficult. We were talking about turning around an organization that for decades seemed to have tried not to win.

The people of New Orleans deserved a great home team, and we were going to give it to them. You can't do that by just hoping for change.

We had to live within the rules of the NFL. We weren't going to ignore them. But we were committed to reviving

a football team and doing what we could to revive a decimated city—even if it meant exhausting ourselves. Some of
the players from that 2006 season would tell you that there
were days and weeks they thought there had to be some kind
of rule that prohibited pushing people so hard.

Conceptually, what we were doing wasn't so complicated.
To find a place on this roster, a player had to show three things:
character, toughness and intelligence. Character. Toughness.
Intelligence. Simply stated, these were our core beliefs.

Bill Belichick had instilled something similar in New
England. Bill Parcells did it in Dallas and the other places
he'd been. In those organizations as in ours, there was clear
recognition that football isn't just a game for mindless jocks.
We wanted talented players, of course—people who had the
technical skills to run, catch, throw and scramble. But the
best players, the right players, are always the ones who can
enrich their technique with real inner fortitude, genuine personal qualities that turn talent into greatness.

Character, toughness, intelligence. We told our scouts
explicitly: Be on the lookout for players who have all three.

We wanted players we didn't have to worry about when
they left the building. There are lots of temptations in New
Orleans, even after a devastating hurricane. We didn't want
players who would be in the French Quarter every night
till five a.m. We wanted players with the character to know
right from wrong and to conduct their lives by that knowl-
edge. Players like that will mold a team, set high standards
and give the others good reason to achieve.

The same is true with intelligence. We put up a sign in
the locker room. "Smart Players Seldom Do Dumb Things."
This doesn't mean just school smarts. Football intelligence

is something more than that—part instinct, part intuition, a big part paying attention. It really comes down to judgment under pressure. How good are the decisions that you make?

And players must be tough. Whatever their talents, however good their team, a time will come when they are challenged. To overcome an injury. To persevere through defeat. To sacrifice personal glory for a higher cause. We wanted players with the toughness to make that choice and live with it.

It didn't matter if a player had been with the team before we got here, or if he was a highly anticipated draft choice, or if he had walked in for a tryout off the street. How the players arrived at Airline Drive was unimportant to us. What they did once they got here would determine how bright their future was. Oh, and anyone who wanted to leave was more than welcome to do so.

For locker room credibility, the starkness of that was huge.

The off-season program began in March with running and weight lifting. That led up to the bonus minicamp in April, which the league allowed all new coaching staffs to hold. Next was the official minicamp at the beginning of June. At each of these turns, we pushed the players extremely hard.

The veterans got their first taste of the new Saints tempo at the April minicamp. We purposely scheduled this before the draft, in order to gain more insight into the roster we'd inherited. The moment the opening horn blasted, the players immediately knew they had never attended a minicamp quite like this, nothing as fast and demanding.

In near-unison, a dozen coaches began to shout orders. But Joe Vitt's South Jersey sandpaper was somehow the loudest of all.

"Get your ass over here," he was yelling. "This isn't a country club. We're not gonna get our asses kicked like we have in the past. Not gonna happen. Not as long as I'm here."

This was not gentle persuasion. This was the earsplitting definition of in-your-face.

Curtis Johnson, our wide receivers coach, was competing with Vitt for oxygen. From Joe Horn on down, all of the players seemed to understand that things were different now.

We didn't give anyone any time for bad body language or stray opinions. It was law and order around here. No Lay-Z-Boys and no lazy boys. The evaluation process had begun.

In early June, the rookies arrived on Airline Drive. We kept going, and we were going hard. The rookies knew immediately they were behind where the veterans were.

By and large, most of the team seemed to grasp the new expectations. There were some exceptions. Donté Stallworth, the Saints' first-round draft pick in 2002 and thirteenth overall that year, showed up late for mandatory team meetings more than once. I had a word with Donté after the second time. "I'm dying to trade or cut you," I told him. "You're making it easy for me."

Donté had been a player who'd flashed signs of greatness—superior speed and some big play-making ability. But his career to that point had been plagued by inconsistency and injuries. And he wasn't doing much to reverse the impression that he was a slacker. In this new Saints offense, someone who was unreliable would have a hard time fitting in.

Defensive tackle Jonathan Sullivan was another player who showed up on the radar—and not in a good way. He too was a first-round pick, sixth overall, the Saints had traded up for in 2003. That meant we had given up two first-round picks to draft this player. He was overweight now and didn't seem eager to expend much extra effort. There was an unfortunate echo here. Earlier in his career, he'd been caught bellying up to the buffet in the pressroom, scooping up hot dogs on a game day. The media had had a blast with that. He too had flashed some signs of promise—and way too many signs of falling short.

Both players were soon on other rosters.

Drew Brees was another story entirely. He got to work immediately, showing himself to be precisely the kind of leader we thought we'd found. With his slowly healing shoulder, he wouldn't be able to throw a football until the end of July. But in mid-April, when the first minicamp started, he refused to stand on the sidelines and just watch. He called the plays in the huddle. He went to the line of scrimmage. He established the cadence. He didn't take the snaps: The other quarterbacks got the reps and threw the balls. But Drew was a key presence in practice from the very start. He was already beginning to develop a rapport with the team. He just didn't throw at first.

His shoulder was only starting to mend. But his leadership was never impaired. In the huddle, in the locker room, in the weight room, in the meetings—he understood exactly what we were trying to do. He got it. He was still new to the program, but he was already one of the main leaders of the team. And this was a locker room full of people trying to find themselves. There were veterans from the old regime. There were new players who'd just shown up. People were just getting to know one another. There was a lot going on here. But Drew was always highly regimented, and he pushed himself and the others around him extraordinarily hard. He had a routine. He stuck with it. It set a powerful example.

When practice was over for the day, he would remain on the

field with several other players and go back through the practice from start to finish, going over whatever repetitions he'd
missed. He did everything at a full-speed tempo except throw.

All the while, we were assessing everyone: people on our
team as well as all the players on the other thirty-one teams.
Every team in the league has a pro-scouting department. We
took the grades and reports from ours very seriously. Who
was still out there that we could maybe grab now? How
did they compare to the guys we had in the building? Do
they have qualities that might be the right addition for the
Saints? We often talked to our players about this process. It
was important for everyone to understand: "Don't just look
closely at our own depth chart. You're not competing with
just the players who are already here. The final fifty-three-
man roster could well include players who are now on other
teams. What you put on tape is your résumé."

Clearly, Drew Brees was at the center of this team we were
building. Others also began to distinguish themselves in a
positive light.

Deuce McAllister, who was recovering from major knee
surgery he'd had the year before, had a limited role in the
off-season, much like Drew. "Much of the Saints' future,"
the sports analysts said, "will depend on where Drew and
Deuce are in rehab." That wasn't far from the truth.

Gradually, the roster was changing dramatically. This
isn't uncommon for teams with a new coaching staff. But we
were not only putting a team together, we were establishing
a whole new way of life. We were a football team on permanent fast-forward.

13

GETTING SHOT

WE WERE HAVING A good initial run. We were getting important work accomplished. It had been difficult and demanding, but most of the players were responding. We were changing the culture. We were exhausting everyone. One thing we were learning: When you set super-high standards, some people will actually meet them. And when you see who doesn't, you don't have to continue to waste time on the people who aren't right. We were beginning to get a good grasp on what we had and what we did not.

And this was just minicamp.

But we didn't want to kill these guys. Before we broke for the summer, before we headed off for our official training camp, we decided to take one day and do something different with the team. We needed a break.

Back in the day, a coach might take his players bowling.

A time would come in the long training season. You'd

been pushing the players hard. They were pushing them-
selves harder. Tensions were rising. Nerves were getting raw.
The coaches, the players, the staff—everyone was exhausted.
It was time for a routine buster.

So you'd organize a bowling outing. Or take the team to
play golf. Or maybe just cancel practice. It's a sound, time-
honored coaching technique. It helps the players blow off a
load of steam, clear their heads, maybe bond a little.

Except—let's be honest here. How much head clearing are
eighty NFL players likely to do in a bowling alley? How much
bonding will million-dollar athletes really achieve across
eighteen fairways? How much steam will hard-charging,
testosterone-fueled headbangers blow off on a free Tuesday?

Who are we kidding? This isn't your father's NFL.

When our guys started getting tired and tense, I knew we
needed a venue that was a little more fitting for their competitive natures, aggressive tendencies and killer instincts.
No offense, Brunswick, but bowling didn't seem like the
answer here.

On this particular morning, our meeting started like it
always did, with the football equivalent of roll call on a cop
show. An inspirational message. An overview of that day's
practice plans. Some logistical directions before we hit the
field. On this day, as on many others, the lights were lowered
and a PowerPoint presentation came up.

Only this was not the usual morning-meeting PowerPoint
presentation. It was the opening battle scene from *Saving
Private Ryan*. It's Omaha Beach, June 6, 1944. There's a
crazy firefight and—you remember—the guy pulls out a little
mirror. He's using the mirror to get the location of a Ger-
man soldier. At the end of the day, the Americans are able

to advance, but under heavy fire. It's twenty-five minutes of some of the most intense moviemaking you ever saw.

The clip ended, and I spoke to the team.

"Our staff works hard," I said. "They work hard to make sure we are covering everything. We can prepare you for the two-minute offense and the red zone and third down. But at some point, you'll have to get into these battles yourselves. You'll have to depend on each other. Your talent, your training and each other—that's where your strength will come from."

Just then, big globs of paint splattered across the video screens. Red, blue, black, followed by the words "Paintball Command"—a paintball company across Lake Pontchartrain in Mandeville. Then two columns of players' names. Those were the black and the gold paintball teams.

As the meeting was continuing, our equipment staff was in the locker room, distributing a pair of sweatpants and a long-sleeved T-shirt to every player. Half got black ones. Half got gold. All this was done quietly during the meeting. And five buses pulled into the parking lot, each with an armed instructor who'd be riding with the players to Mandeville to brief them on what was coming next.

As soon as the video screens went dark, Steve Gleason, Drew Brees and some of the others started painting their faces. You could tell this was going to be competitive. We weren't even on the buses yet.

It's a forty-five-minute ride from our practice facility to the paintball place. Along the way, the instructors showed the players how to load the paint pellets, how to aim the rifles and how to shoot. They explained the rules of engagement and what constitutes a kill. "These are weapons," the instructor on our bus said. "Please don't be shooting each other from three feet away."

Paintball Command is not somewhere you would just stumble on. It's off a highway, down a gravel road through the woods. You make a left and then a right. You have to want to find it. On the property, there are a few modulars with cash registers and a staging area. There's a grove, where later we'd eat oysters and barbecue and give out awards. But when we drove up, the layout really did seem like some military-ops location. There were a bunch of old wooden spools. There was black mesh netting just hanging there. The place looked like something you'd see in upstate Washington, maybe, or some militant skinhead outpost. It was big. It was all spread out. There were lots of trees. There was a huge wooden fort that you knew at some point one team would be defending and the other team would be trying to take.

The CO_2 canisters were already in the paint guns. The paintball pellets were stacked in bags near the guns. We had everything we needed for a long drawn-out firefight. I think we went through about $6,000 worth of ammo that day.

We played defend the hill. We played capture the flag. The gold team attacked. The black team defended. In the next scenario, the roles were turned around. When you got hit, an official would wave his flag, declaring you dead. But you could go inside, recharge and return to fight again.

Under any circumstances, paintball is a raucous activity. But when the combatants are highly competitive professional athletes finally freed from their protocols after months of rigorous training—well, the firefights quickly took on a crazed, frantic edge. And the rules of engagement—what rules of engagement? Mammoth linemen—320, 340 pounds—coming at one another, guns blazing. Wily special teams guys, seeking every advantage. Brees in face paint. Scott Fujita barking orders. Reggie Bush totally wild-eyed. Paint was everywhere. The coaches were as bloody as anyone.

Me? I had my little setup in the fort—very protected, a spot I was sure wasn't vulnerable. I had a couple of bags of ammo. I was the sniper I had always imagined myself to be. I managed to hit a few people and stay pretty clean.

At some point, I bent slightly to my left to lift some ammo—and wham! A solid hit on my shoulder.

Somebody got me.

I scanned the bushes quickly. There was safety Steve Gleason, who had been waiting patiently for the shot.

"I got him," Gleason yelled, laughing. "I got him. I was waiting forever for that!"

This was perfect. Gleason was one of the players we had inherited from the old regime. He'd been a Saint since 2000. And although he didn't have the size or the speed or the paper credentials of some other defensive backs, he had something more important than any of that: He had the heart. He had the drive and the passion and the dedication to get it done, whatever *it* was. When I had first gotten to the Saints and met him, I thought he was an employee, not a player. He was a true special teams guy. Three months later, in one of the greatest moments in New Orleans Saints history, he would block the first punt against the Atlanta Falcons in our return to the Superdome. There's a player on the team now just like him, Chris Reis, who recovered the onside kick that was called an ambush in Super Bowl XLIV. These are players who deserve every success they've had.

The paintball battle continued for another ninety minutes, nothing but paint pellets flying through the woods. Black on gold. Gold on black. And lots of friendly fire.

When the war finally ended, we all went back to the grove to eat. We gave awards to the players for their performance in the off-season program. Most improved. Biggest lifter. Perfect attendance. As a memento of the day, they all got Bose iPod docks.

It was hot. This was June in Louisiana. After a full-throttle, two-hour firefight, I think every one of them had lost ten pounds. I'm sure we burned through more calories than we would have on the practice field.

So much for the day off.

There was a moment when we were finished eating lunch, just enjoying the watermelon, when I looked around at these players and thought: "These guys may be highly trained athletes. They are also little kids."

To this day, some of the players still have a scar, a nick or some other souvenir they can point to on their body and say, "This is from that paintball game in '06." The pellets were made to be shot from twenty yards, not two feet. So the next day in the locker room, our players looked like some horrible dermatological experiment gone wrong. Everyone had two or three major bruises.

What made the day so special wasn't just how hard they had fought the paintball battles. It was how hard they had worked in March, April and May. We had gotten on them. We had not let up. We practiced at a pace most of them had never experienced before. And that gave paintball, at that late point in the process, a near-mythic impact.

And it cut across every line.

On a normal day, the assistant coaches might spend 90 or 95 percent of their time with their own position group. The D line coach with the defensive line and the running back coach with the running backs. There's some interaction with the other players in the locker room, but not a lot. When you do something like this, you get to know some other players and coaches a little more intimately than you had known them before the day began.

It was an experience. It was something the guys would always talk about. We were bonding and creating memories here. It wasn't just the finish line we were going for. This was something we learned eventually at the Super Bowl. The journey was just as important as the getting there.

14

GETTING WET

MICKEY AND I BOTH felt like it would be good to take this year's training camp out of town. This wouldn't be the first time the Saints had gone away for camp. Training camp had been held in several different places. The team had been to Thibodaux in southwest Louisiana. They'd gone as far as Wisconsin. And many years, camp was held right on Airline Drive. But in the summer of 2006, we believed, there were too many distractions in New Orleans. Too many things still weren't working right. If we were expecting these players to devote themselves 100 percent to football, we knew a little distance couldn't hurt.

We would serve New Orleans better, I thought, by briefly getting away.

I liked the idea of setting up training camp on a small college campus where everything we needed could be self-contained. Away from the city but not too far away. "Let's look at a radius of a couple hours," I told Mickey. "Maybe there's a place we can find."

We visited the University of Louisiana at Lafayette. We visited Southeastern and Northeastern. We'd heard about Millsaps in Jackson, Mississippi. The team had another reason for sending us out on this Gulf-region campus-scouting tour. We were doing a PR deal with Mr. Benson to help generate season-ticket sales. We flew up to Shreveport and made an announcement about an upcoming preseason game. Then we flew over to Jackson. While we were there, we had a chance to look at the facilities at Millsaps. We loved what we saw.

Millsaps College was Old South. Founded in 1889 and affiliated with the United Methodist Church, the school has a lovely campus on the edge of downtown Jackson, surrounded by a tall iron fence. I liked the fact that it was just two hours from New Orleans. But I especially liked the fact that here was an entire universe cut off from the many distractions of outside life. Where the players would sleep, where we'd all eat, where we'd hold our meetings, where we'd practice—all that was in close proximity. Millsaps was a place where you could put your dorm key on a shoelace and not worry about anything except the things you were supposed to be worrying about. I don't know if our players that summer would describe it the same way. But the campus seemed ideal for a brutally tough New Orleans Saints training camp.

The fields were beat up a little. One had a slope. And the dorms were old. The beds were so small, I wasn't sure how a football player could squeeze into one. We came up with an arrangement and placed a large order with a bedding company: In every room, there were two double box springs with a queen mattress on top. It looked a little ridiculous, like a multilayered wedding cake with sheets and blankets. But it worked.

The players understood training camp was going to be hot. This was late July in Mississippi. What did they expect? But I asked the college maintenance chief to keep the inside temperature as low as he possibly could. It might be an oven on the practice field, but I wanted a deep freeze inside.

This would keep the players from dozing off in the meetings after a long day on the field.

The maintenance man lowered all the thermostats—the players would say to 61 or 62 degrees in the meeting rooms, in the dorms, everywhere we were that was inside. I blamed this on the maintenance crew in the same breath I was telling the director: "Thanks. It's perfect." Dan Dalrymple, our strength coach who weighs about 340 pounds, claimed he had frost on his windows. Dan was exaggerating. But watching him climb on his bed was a treat. Players, coaches, everyone—we all wore sweatshirts inside.

When a professional team arrives on campus and sets up a training camp, the relationship with the college can be a little dicey. The college administrators like the activity. They appreciate the income. But we're using their facilities. Maybe the staff and the students are inconvenienced. From the president on down, people at the college can sometimes ask, "Is it really worth the headaches? We don't need to be the summer landlord of an NFL team." But the character of our players seemed to matter. The people at Millsaps, the people in greater Jackson—they kept coming up and telling me, "We love your team. They are such good guys. Coach, we love the players you're signing. They're respectful in the cafeteria. They'll sign autographs. Please keep coming here."

One thing was obvious: The people at Millsaps were totally committed to making everything right. They were awesome.

Certainly, we were pushing hard on the practice fields, harder even than we had on Airline Drive. This was a new level of brutal practice. Running and hitting. Running some more. Full-pad practices twice a day in the Mississippi sun. Really, what choice did we have? This team was going to have to be in excellent shape to win in this league.

It was difficult. It was drudgery. It was stiflingly hot.

And practice was never rained out. The big joke at training camp was that it rained often in the humid Jackson summer—but it never seemed to rain until our practice was done. It was as if we had made some deal with the devil.

"This is like that movie *The Truman Show*," I told the media one day. "We are controlling the rain to fit our schedule. Nothing gets in the way of our practice."

The way our players were practicing, they could have fallen asleep on a big pile of jagged bricks. Those wedding cake beds never looked so good.

The first question each day was always, "How hot is the turf going to be at nine a.m.?" That's where we started practice every morning. That's where I wanted our first conditioning test to be.

One morning, our head trainer, Scottie Patton, came over to me. He had the little heat index. He said, "Sean, the heat index is 128 right now."

You have to understand the role of a head trainer. Their job is to worry. Scottie had been dealing with the IVs each day. The temperatures weren't getting any cooler. Players used to say they saw no birds flying over Jackson, only low-buzzing horseflies.

Mainly what we did was practice and practice some more.

In the years since that summer, our players have never forgotten that training camp. Complaints about our stay there are an ingrained part of New Orleans Saints folklore. It was something that everyone suffered through together. We were laying a foundation for what was coming next.

The back-and-forth became like a ritual.

"Hey, Coach," someone would say, "cold enough in here for you? You think maybe we could get 'em to lower it a few more degrees before the meeting starts?"

"I wanted it cold," I'd bark. "It's cold, all right?"

And we were seeing progress.

Gradually, but only gradually, the strength was returning to Drew Brees's arm and Deuce McAllister's knee. We were all impatient, of course—no one more than Drew and Deuce. We watched them both closely and tried to measure each day's progress. In practice one day, I told Pete Carmichael, the quarterbacks coach: "There doesn't seem to be a lot of velocity with Drew's passing. Is this what we're getting?"

Pete was the only coach who could compare Drew's velocity to how it was before the injury when they'd worked together in San Diego.

"No, no, Coach," Pete assured me. "It's not looking good right now. But this isn't it. This isn't his arm strength at all."

Just say we were concerned.

Midway through training camp, we saw Drew and Deuce

begin to get better. In Drew's case, his timing started to click. Deuce was beginning to move more quickly on his surgically repaired knee. Both of them were making visible progress. But would it be enough? And would it be in time?

This was Training Camp 101. There was nothing about it that was easy. I asked Joe Vitt: "Do we go tomorrow in pads, or do we back off?"

That was a dumb question to ask Joe Vitt.

"We keep fuckin' going full pads," he said. That was always Vitt's message. Always. It wasn't until I heard his tone change that we all began to wonder: Maybe we needed to back off a little.

The results we were seeing could not be ignored. These players were getting stronger. More important, they were getting tougher. Even the coaches were starting to get some rhythm here. This was the first time most of these guys had ever coached together. They too were becoming a team.

But it was becoming obvious, the importance of occasional breaks. Everyone needed a break. Not necessarily paintball. Something a little cooler maybe. A training camp excursion more appropriate for the Mississippi heat. These breaks would become as crucial to the curriculum as block-and-tackle drills and wind sprints.

Twenty-five minutes outside Jackson, there was a water park. The owner is a big Saints fan. He agreed to shut down the park on a Wednesday. He said he'd leave the concession stand open with pizza, burgers and cold drinks. It would just be us. Again, we kept the trip a surprise.

"I do not want word getting out," I told the coaches in our staff meeting. Everyone got assignments. One coach coordinated the buses. Someone else led the start of practice. Someone slipped shorts and towels into every player's locker while the team was on the field. Again, every detail mattered.

These guys had put up with a whole lot of punishment. But by now, they were approaching the point of mutiny. I know I didn't feel like walking any planks. First thing in the morning, the coaches led them through the usual stretches and warm-ups. Then we pulled everyone up. I gave them some long-winded speech that transitioned gradually into the important of temperature control.

"You guys ever been to a water park before?" I asked.

You'd be surprised how many players didn't raise their hands. Just like paintball, these were new experiences for many of them.

The players sprinted inside. They got the shorts and towels from their lockers. We were on the buses in five minutes.

We had made the trip mandatory. Had it been presented as optional, it would have been just me and the coaches and our inner tubes. Many of the players would have retired to their wedding cakes for naps.

When we pulled up and they saw the wave pool, lazy river and all the water-park bells and whistles, they were a team of six-year-olds again.

After three hours, it was nearing time to leave. There was this one slide at the south end of the park that had caught everyone's eye. This was the high dive of water slides, about four stories up with wooden steps and a long flume at the bottom.

The players devised a contest—offense versus defense, five men from each side. Which side could slide the farthest?

The winning team would get an extra hour of curfew Friday night. Two weeks into a training camp, an extra hour of curfew was like gold bullion.

Immediately, the players began to strategize. Was it size? Was it weight? Which five players would be the best? Like any group of children, they had trouble deciding. Everything was up for grabs. Eventually, the offense had its five. So did the defense. One by one, the players climbed the wooden stairs to the top. One by one, they came flying down.

But one fact was becoming apparent. If you went down the slide immediately after the slider before you, you'd end up sliding a little farther at the end. Some of the water would have splashed from the flume, and the slide wouldn't have filled up yet. Four inches of water produces less drag than eight.

Scott Fujita was cleanup for the defense. Fujita's from Southern California. He's linear, six foot five. He's a surfer dude.

Charles Grant had just gone before him. Their strategy was brilliant. Grant wasn't going to hit the mark for him. Grant's job was to take his three-hundred-pound frame and displace as much of the water as possible.

Fujita followed in Grant's wake, easily beating any of the previous bests. On the field and off, the players were learning to cooperate.

Saints executive vice president/ general manager Mickey Loomis believed in me and gave me my first head coaching job. In four short years, we reached the pinnacle of our professions when we were able to hoist the Vince Lombardi Trophy together.

U2's the Edge (LEFT) and Bono (RIGHT) surrounding Green Day's Billie Joe Armstrong lead the emotional sellout crowd in a rousing rendition of "The Saints Are Coming" prior to our homecoming kickoff on September 25, 2006.

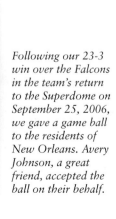

Following our 23-3 win over the Falcons in the team's return to the Superdome on September 25, 2006, we gave a game ball to the residents of New Orleans. Avery Johnson, a great friend, accepted the ball on their behalf.

Pro Football Hall of Famer Ronnie Lott, who spoke to our team during the season, coined the phrase "Smell Greatness." I'm proud to say that we followed his advice.

Ben Sarrat Jr., who suffered from a terminal illness and sadly passed away shortly after our Super Bowl victory, is seen here on the sideline with me before we played the New York Jets on October 4, 2009. He was an inspiration to our entire team.

Saints' vice president of communications Greg Bensel and I walking off the field prior to our game in Atlanta. Greg and I work closely together, and he is a trusted adviser.

Following our team's 38-17 win over the New England Patriots on Monday Night Football on November 22 at the Superdome, I was joined postgame by my agent, Don Yee (FAR LEFT), ESPN analyst Jon Gruden, Kenny Chesney, and ESPN play-by-play announcer Mike Tirico.

Pregame against the Washington Redskins on December 6, 2009, Drew Brees (#9) and I discussed our game plan. We ended up winning the game in overtime 33-30 and securing the NFC South Championship.

My "consigliere," Joe Vitt, and marketing agent Mike Ornstein celebrate clinching the NFC South in Washington on December 6, 2009. I rely heavily on these two men.

(LEFT TO RIGHT) *Saints owner Tom Benson, owner/executive vice president Rita Benson LeBlanc, Gayle Benson, and I celebrate our clinching the NFC South Championship in our locker room at Washington on December 6, 2009.*

(LEFT TO RIGHT) *On our flight home from Washington, Assistant Head Coach/Linebacker Coach Joe Vitt, Defensive Coordinator Gregg Williams, and I listen to a voice mail on my cell phone left by my former high school teammate Joe Imparato. It's a tradition that Imparato leaves his "pregame" speeches on my cell before our games.*

After we defeated the Minnesota Vikings 31-28, in the NFC Championship Game at the Superdome on January 24, 2010, Jimmy Buffett (LEFT) and Kenny Chesney proudly display the Halas Trophy, which is awarded to the NFC champions.

After our plane from New Orleans arrived in Miami, I rushed ahead of the team buses and quickly changed into bellmen's clothing. Our players who had responsibilities at the Pro Bowl the night before were already there to welcome our team to the hotel. (LEFT TO RIGHT): Jonathan Vilma, Roman Harper, Jahri Evans, Jonathan Goodwin, Jon Stinchcomb, and Drew Brees. It loosened the mood quite a bit and helped set the tone for a big week of preparation for our entire traveling party.

Due to inclement weather upon our arrival in Miami, we bused north to the Dolphins indoor practice facility for a practice. Drew Brees (#9), Bill Parcells, and Hall of Fame finalist Cortez Kennedy joined me for a quick photo after practice.

We conducted a morning walk-through in the grand ballroom of the team's headquarters Hotel Intercontinental before departing for practice.

During our Super Bowl practices at the University of Miami, I wore clothing from the "U" since they were such great hosts to our team. Here I am chatting with CBS Sports analyst Bill Cowher at our Thursday practice. Cowher was one of the very few people who picked us to win the game.

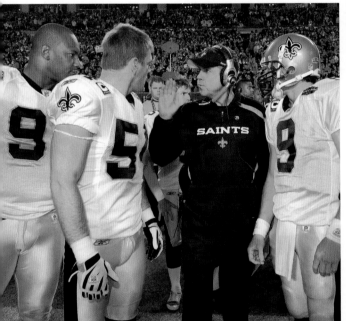

Prior to the coin toss in Super Bowl XLIV, I gathered our team captains Will Smith (#91), Troy Evans (#54), and Drew Brees (#9). Jonathan Vilma (#51) was warming up on the field.

A big reason why winning Super Bowl XLIV was so special is that I was able to share it with my son, Connor, my daughter, Meghan, and my wife, Beth. That's us doing a pregame "fist bump." And that's us about an hour and a half before kickoff when they joined me on our sideline. This one was extra-special for us.

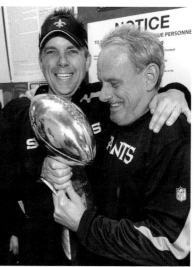

Moments after the game, I was presented with the Vince Lombardi Trophy. It was one of many kisses to be planted on it that night.

Joe Vitt has been a coach in the National Football League for more than thirty years. This was his first opportunity to hold the Lombardi Trophy, and it was certainly well deserved. Joe is a tremendous coach and motivator, and it was special to witness his reaction.

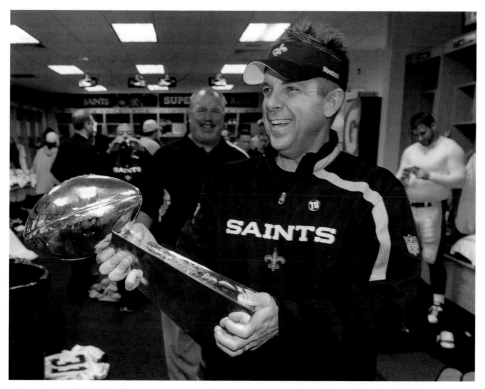

After we finally left the field following Super Bowl XLIV, it was great to spend time with our team in the winning locker room.

Our postgame Super Bowl XLIV victory party featured Kenny Chesney, and his rendition of "Living in Fast Forward" never sounded sweeter than it did with the Vince Lombardi Trophy accompanying him onstage.

The flight from Miami to New Orleans wasn't a particularly long one, so catching a quick nap came easily. Of course, the Vince Lombardi Trophy wasn't far from my grip.

The victory parade that was held in the Saints' honor upon our return from Super Bowl XLIV was extraordinary. The crowd was estimated to be more than eight hundred thousand people, and the view from atop my float was overwhelming.

15

TEST DRIVE

IT WAS TIME TO take this team for a test drive.

But so much wasn't ready yet, and I don't just mean Drew's shoulder or Deuce's knee. While we'd been working frantically to rebuild a football team, a parallel campaign was beginning to pick up speed, the earliest rebuilding of some crucial parts of New Orleans. By midsummer, huge amounts were still undone. Lakeview, Broadmoor, the Ninth Ward, certainly the Mississippi Gulf Coast, were not moving nearly as quickly as people had hoped for. But some actual pockets of success could now be identified. Many of the downtown hotels and many of the larger restaurants were open again, even if major convention business was now a distant memory. The French Quarter—the city's historic jewel, which hadn't flooded at all—looked almost the same as it always had. And as insurance checks were slowly reaching homeowners and a big rush of immigrant laborers arrived, the glorious sound of hammers and power tools could be heard in neighborhoods like Uptown, Marigny and Gentilly, in Metairie and on the West Bank. The Superdome was still a work in progress. As the shelter of last resort, it had taken Katrina hard. But the reports we were getting from Poydras Avenue said genuine progress was being made. The state officials overseeing the massive project had been amazingly focused. Mr. Benson, the NFL commissioner's office, and even city hall were pitching in. Everyone seemed to understand. If the Saints were going to remain New Orleans' home team, they had to have someplace to play.

And soon.

Since we didn't have our stadium back yet, our four preseason games had to be played outside New Orleans. Two of those were considered home games, despite the far-flung geography. We played the Dallas Cowboys in the northern Louisiana city of Shreveport and hosted the Indianapolis Colts right across the street from the Millsaps campus at Jackson Memorial Stadium.

Shreveport is actually closer to Dallas than to New Orleans. For decades, that was Cowboys country. There were some Saints fans in North Louisiana in the late summer of 2006, though not nearly as many as there are today. Still, it made a lot of sense to bring a preseason Cowboys-Saints game to Shreveport. Both teams had a claim on the region. The rivalry was real. The tickets sold briskly. Turnout for the game was strong. And it wasn't like the Dome was ready anyway.

That preseason "home" game was my first chance to coach against Bill Parcells. I'd been his assistant, of course, the previous three years in Dallas. And this wouldn't be the only Saints-Cowboys matchup of 2006. We had a regular-season game on the schedule for Week Fourteen at Dallas. But this first matchup was like a rite of passage for me.

Which made the lopsided results even more embarrassing. We got our butts kicked that night by the Cowboys, 30-7.

Now, I knew this was only preseason. But when you come out of a game like that, you have to say to yourself, "It wasn't that we didn't play our starters. It wasn't that we were still learning our plays. Regardless of what we had done, it wouldn't have mattered. They thumped us. Badly."

Preseason results don't count in any official way. But understand this: In preseason, you can gain or lose confidence. Clearly this was a game we viewed as a setback.

I sat in the locker room with Mickey, right before we got on the buses. It was just Mickey and me. Feeling dejected, I turned to him and said flat-out, "We might not win three games this year."

I half believed that.

After what we'd just shown on the field in Shreveport, Mickey couldn't argue. "Hey, you wanted to be the head coach," he said.

On this whole ride, that was the emotional low point for me, my moment of greatest pessimism. We'd worked so hard all summer. We'd sweated and strained and slept on wedding cake beds. And we still had so far to go. It was frustrating, downright maddening. Of the two teams we'd just seen on the field, one was so much further along in its growth. The Cowboys were bigger and better, and they'd been on Parcells's program in '03, '04, '05 and now in '06—four years of systematic improvement. It showed. We were at the very beginning of our journey.

But we didn't sit around feeling sorry for ourselves. No one wanted to hear about our labor pains. Instead, we just got busier, trying to improve the team. What choice did we have? Parcells had already preached that success was a journey. It doesn't come instantly. But one way to avoid it for sure was to give up the hunt.

A week after the Dallas disappointment, we traded for Scott Shanle, who had been part of the Cowboys team that had whipped us. He started immediately for us at weak-side linebacker, where he's been a huge asset for the past four years.

We also made a trade with Philadelphia for Mark Simoneau. He jumped into the middle linebacker position. Remember what I said about other people's rosters? We needed to upgrade at linebackers. Obtaining two starters one week before the regular season was an over-the-top example of that. By this time, Donté Stallworth and Jonathan Sullivan were long gone.

The game in Jackson, our third in the preseason, was against the Indianapolis Colts. We lost 27-14. But it wasn't the score or even the loss I remember most vividly. It was an interception that Drew Brees threw. That concerned me. The ball just floated over our receiver's head and into the hands of the Colts' cornerback. That ball was begging, pleading, almost demanding to be intercepted. And the play was a jarring reminder that Drew's shoulder was not fully healed. There were a couple of other throws as well in that game that gave all of us pause. We didn't lose faith in Drew. We had seen real progress. And it wasn't like we had a long list of viable alternatives at quarterback. We had no plan B at all.

What would we have done when the real season began if Drew wasn't ready? Probably run a lot of handoffs, that's all.

Nothing needed to be said out loud by Drew, by Pete Carmichael or by me. We all knew there was work to be done. The healing process wasn't finished. The problem was we were running short on time.

Really, what could anybody say? There was still way too much positive energy coming from Drew. It was never a question of "Is the shoulder going to be healthy?" The question for Drew was "What's the growth potential and how much better will you continue to get?"

And others were stepping up, especially some of the rookies we'd chosen behind Reggie Bush in the draft. A seventh-round draft pick from Hofstra University named Marques Colston was beginning to shine. Throughout training camp, he got better with every practice. The progress he'd shown had made us comfortable trading the erratic Donté Stallworth to Philadelphia. Jahri Evans, our fourth-round selection from Bloomsburg State, was winning a battle to start at right guard. Roman Harper, the second-round selection from Alabama, was doing the same at strong safety. And among the veterans, Deuce McAllister was making real strides. His knee, injured the year before, was really beginning to heal now. What a backfield pair he and Reggie would make! All these players, just like Reggie, would end up being key contributors for us in the years to come. That draft class was spectacular.

Not by accident, our first two games of the regular season were also being played on the road. The Superdome was in the final month of its overhaul. For the first time, people were saying with confidence that the reopening deadline would be met.

We opened the regular season in Cleveland, beating the

Browns 19-14. Nothing flashy but a win nonetheless. Drew had finally turned the corner. Although he wasn't 100 percent, there was a huge feeling of relief on the coaching staff, even from Drew himself. I think if you asked him, "At what point in 2006 did you feel 100 percent healthy?" he would tell you, "Shortly after that opening game, in Week Two or Week Three."

For the second game of the season, we traveled to Green Bay, Wisconsin, and historic Lambeau Field, one of the best venues anywhere in the sports world. I swear, the whole time I wasn't thinking, "What if...?" The stadium is nestled in a residential neighborhood, not some anonymous suburb or high-rise downtown. The parking lot smells of bratwurst and barbecue. The fans arrive hours before game time. Friendly tailgating is like a religion there. They'll say, "Welcome to our stadium. Let us tell you about our traditions." There's a warm feeling—to some degree that exists in New Orleans as well. Green Bay is just a unique and special place—one reason I'd kept checking my cell phone in New Orleans that night on my way to dinner with Mickey.

But despite Green Bay's tradition and cheerfulness, we still had to worry about Brett Favre and a very good Packers team. We came back from an early deficit and won that game 34-27. It was the first of many comebacks orchestrated by Drew Brees.

The victory meant something to us. With an outpouring of second-half effort, we'd come from behind to win our second game in a row on the road. Starting out 2-0 after two road games is a big accomplishment for any team in our league. And every bit as important as that final score was that Drew had made two or three throws in that game that reminded Pete Carmichael of the healthy quarterback he knew in San Diego.

"I'm seeing it," Pete said.

Our defense was showing signs of improvement as well. And the results were rolling in. If we could pull out a third victory the following weekend in New Orleans, that would equal the entire sum total of the previous year's wins.

16

WELCOME DOME

IT WAS ONLY THE biggest game in New Orleans Saints history—a game many people thought would never be played.

The date was September 25, 2006, not quite thirteen months after Katrina. So much was still up in the air. Would the local economy recover? Would more people move back? Would the levees hold? Could the Superdome ever be a place of celebration again? As the first Saints home game got closer, the answers were as murky as the floodwaters had been.

But this much was clear: The Dome would be ready. The Falcons would be here. The game would be on *Monday Night Football*.

The rivalry with Atlanta went back to the earliest days of the Saints. But the matchup had never been this intense. Both teams were 2-0. Atlanta certainly looked strong. They had just come off a franchise record 306 rushing yards against

Tampa Bay. Jim L. Mora—whose dad, Jim Mora, was the most successful coach in Saints history—was coaching the Falcons. They had a talented quarterback named Michael Vick. But we had momentum too. We'd won two games already. If we beat Atlanta, we'd have won as many—one, two, three—as the team had in the entire last season. These Saints were different, and here was early proof. This was the fans' first chance to get an in-person view of Drew Brees, Reggie Bush and this new team we were building. It was a huge public event in a place that hadn't been having many of those. For the people of New Orleans, this night was part football game and part recovery pep rally—a chance to tell the world, "Don't count this team out yet—or this city." And playing an ESPN *Monday Night Football* game, we were sure to have a giant national audience.

And, frankly, I wasn't sure our players were prepared.

How could they be? Half our guys had never played in the Dome before. That included all the first- and second-year players. And nobody at all had played in the Dome since its top-to-bottom renovation, a whirlwind $193 million job. The lighting was different. The surface was new. The sound and video systems were now state-of-the-art. This was really a brand-new stadium inside an old shell, and there was no denying that the place was sparkling. But anything so different will take some getting used to. And God only knew what ghosts were lurking there.

Thirty thousand people had taken refuge in the Superdome when they'd had no place else to go. All of our players had heard the stories and seen the TV reports. It was hot and dark those days, and the smell was bad. Food and water and medicine were scarce. Babies cried and fistfights broke out. Along with the Morial Convention Center, it really had been the shelter of last resort. Some of the worst rumors had turned out to be exaggerated. No one had actually been murdered in the Superdome after Katrina. But one man had committed suicide, and nobody had been left unscathed. And when the people did finally get out of there, most of them were shipped off to further heartbreak and despair. Even a year and a month later, images like that can mess with a player's head.

I discussed all this with the coaches, and they quickly agreed: We had to do something to ease the players back into the Dome. Why not hold Friday's practice there?

My concern for this game was not us being ready or energized. This was *Monday Night Football* against Atlanta, back home in New Orleans, both teams 2-0. The buzz was guaranteed. My concern was us being too tight, too distracted, too emotionally wound up—and having our execution suffer. I wanted to deal with all of that before game time.

We had to try to chase the ghosts away.

Everywhere I went that week, I could feel the excitement rising. The Saints were back in New Orleans. They were playing in the Superdome. After a year with little to cheer about, that was something right there.

The energy kept getting more intense. I could only imagine how loud the fans would be. But I could not let the team forget what their primary job was here: We were playing to win a football game. We'd worked too hard to lose our concentration. I brought this up with the players at Thursday's practice.

"Monday has a chance to be a special night," I told them. "It's going to be a memorable night regardless of the outcome. But it will be a special night only if we win."

None of this "We're just happy to be here," OK?

"The coaches and I, we know you're going to be ready," I told them. "But this game will come down to you being able to focus, much like a play-off game or a Super Bowl. Both teams will be ready. Now, will you keep your focus with the increased atmosphere and distractions and media coverage and all the other things that go into this game?

"I am counting on it."

On Friday, everyone had a chance to check out the new locker rooms, to stare into the new field lights, to bounce up and down on the Sportexe Momentum turf. This wasn't just a walk-though. It was an actual practice. We started at the same time the game was starting on Monday. We practiced plays we were working on. We did our usual exercises and drills. I wanted the players to experience as much as possible what they would experience on Monday night.

After we were finished practicing, I had everyone gather on the fifty-yard line. The players were sweaty in their pads and uniforms. I introduced Doug Thornton. A former Shreveport oilman and an ex–college quarterback from McNeese State, Doug had stayed in the Dome around the clock through the entire Katrina ordeal. Then he was the person in charge of renovating the Dome. "He did a phenomenal job getting this done on time," I told the players. "It was an amazing task. We owe him. He's been a tremendous ally to all of us."

I introduced Benny Vanderklis, who was in charge of security and had also ridden out the storm. I wanted the team to recognize and appreciate what all these people had been doing and what they had managed to achieve. Then I tapped my hat. That was the signal.

The lights went down. The Dome stayed dark for a moment.

Then both the new Jumbotrons lit up, and a powerful high-lights video filled the screens. Not the kind of highlights that usually play before a football game. These were highlights of Katrina. Lowlights may be a better word.

The video was just five minutes long. But I swear, it was the most emotional five minutes of tape I'd ever seen. The rising water, the people's faces, the houses with X's on the doors let-ting the rescuers know how many bodies were inside. Those thick New Orleans accents. Very, very powerful stuff from beginning to end. And when the video was finished, these images of Katrina gave way to a song—the throaty exuber-ance of Hank Williams Jr. singing "Are You Ready for Some Football?"—the *Monday Night Football* theme.

Talk about a jarring juxtaposition. From "Oh, my God, look at where we've come from" to "Oh, my God, look where we're going now." This was exactly the order it would go in on Monday night.

The players looked stunned. They were just standing there in their pads in silence. I let the emotion seep in. Coaches, players, me—not a word from any of us. It was a huge, emo-tional moment for all of us. We were back in the Dome after all that had happened and getting ready to play. At least we went through it on Friday.

That was exactly what I was hoping for. Three nights later, when we'd all be back in the Dome again, I wanted all of us to be past that part. I wanted the rush of emotion on Friday, not on Monday night. On Monday, this team had to execute.

Because, remember, it's only special if we win.

Monday finally came, and the Superdome literally glowed. The fans were beside themselves with anticipation. Thank-fully, we had a quarterback to put on the field.

We tried to think through every last detail. We even had valet parking for the players. They'd pull up to the Dome, and fifty valets were waiting for them. They'd leave the car with a valet, and their keys would be waiting in their locker at the end of the game. No one had to worry about the parking garage.

Traffic was backed up around the Dome. One by one, the players arrived. A huge crowd of fans watched them walk inside—not down a protected tunnel but along an open chute about twenty yards long and ten feet wide. A few of the players walked straight down the middle between the lines of fans. But most veered either left or right, waving, smiling, high-fiving the fans. Energy was being transferred. The excitement was one thing no one could ignore.

The players were all supposed to be there by six thirty, two hours before the game. Most showed up by five thirty or six. But at six twenty, nobody had seen Drew Brees. This was strange. Drew would normally be a five o'clock guy. He'd get taped, get dressed, do his entire routine. He wasn't someone who liked to rush in.

I was getting concerned. "Where is Drew?" I yelled at Greg Bensel, the PR guy. Greg made a cell phone call. He sent a text. Finally, he had an answer. "He got spun around in his Land Rover, got caught in traffic and got lost," Greg said, looking up from his BlackBerry.

We had to send out a police escort to find our quarterback. They made a path through the traffic and led him to the garage entrance. The valet service had already stopped.

You know how tall those old Land Rovers are? Well, Drew's was so tall, he jammed it into the top of the Super-dome entryway.

This is the most important game in the city's history. It was twenty-five minutes after six. Our starting quarterback had jammed his Land Rover into the parking garage roof. I just hoped this wasn't a sign for the night.

As a player and as a coach, at some point or another, you have that nightmare. The national anthem is being played, and you're two blocks away from the stadium. I knew Drew was dying before the game.

"Hey, Drew," I said, needling him a little when he finally arrived. "Glad you were able to join us tonight."

When game time finally arrived, the Dome was in a frenzy. Katrina had scattered Saints fans everywhere, but 72,968 somehow managed to find their way to the Superdome. It was a spectacular, New Orleans–style event. Cannons shot black-and-gold confetti. Music filled the air. Green Day and U2 performed "Wake Me When September Ends" and "The Saints Are Coming" and a reworked version of "House of the Rising Sun." They showed the Katrina video, and everyone got quiet. The Hank Williams Jr. song came up. "What a pleasure it is to welcome you all back inside the Louisiana Superdome," Mike Tirico told the ESPN audience, which was the network's largest ever for a sporting event.

The feeling inside the Dome was absolutely electric. The symbolism was impossible to ignore. After fifty-six weeks, football was returning to New Orleans. Was it too much to hope the city was also coming back to life? The place was fully awash in emotion.

It was the loudest crowd I'd ever heard in my life. I know I never walked into a stadium feeling like more was riding on the game. The fanfare and the atmosphere were just unbelievable. There were some familiar faces: former President George H. W. Bush, Spike Lee, Harry Connick Jr., Hillary Swank and NFL commissioners Paul Tagliabue and Roger Goodell. Dallas Mavericks head coach Avery Johnson had a sideline pass.

But it was longtime Saints fans at home with their team again.

And not for one single moment did our guys forget why we were there.

The game got off to an amazing start. On the very first possession, the Falcons went three and out and were forced to punt deep in their own territory.

Special teams coordinator John Bonamego had convinced me we had a real good punt-block rush. He gave Steve Gleason, my assassin on paintball day, a specific assignment. This was perfect for Gleason. He didn't have great athletic ability. He didn't have that much speed. At five foot eleven, 212 pounds, he was definitely on the small side for an NFL player. As a football player, he didn't have a lot on paper. But you could give Gleason an assignment, and he just had a way of getting it done. If he hit this just right, he could make a kill like he had at paintball.

I didn't plan on trying to block a punt so early. But Bonamego didn't seem eager to wait. "You want to block the first one?" he asked. I knew we wanted to run the block at some point. Teams rush eight and attempt to block punts all the time. But so soon?

I heard myself say, "Yeah, let's do it."

And we did. Eight guys rushed. Gleason hit the A gap, pulled a little loop stunt and went right up the middle to block the punt. It came off the punter's foot. It hit Gleason.

Curtis Deloatch fell on the ball in the end zone. It was 7-0,

New Orleans. And the roar from the crowd made everything else sound like a whisper.

"I don't think I've ever heard anything in my life louder than that," Gleason said later.

Michael Vick had to agree. "I never in my life heard a crowd roar so loud," Vick said. "It just goes to show the appreciation they have for having the New Orleans Saints back in the Dome, bringing football back to the city. I commend them for that. They deserve it."

By the time the game was over, the Saints had won 23-3. Brees had thrown for 191 yards and the glory was spread all around. Deuce McAllister ran for eighty-one yards on nineteen attempts. Reggie Bush had fifty-three yards on thirteen. John Carney kicked two field goals in the second quarter, including a fifty-one-yarder that inched above the crossbars just as halftime arrived. The Saints' defense held Vick to twelve completions in thirty-one passing attempts. His runs logged a grand total of twenty-seven yards, not counting a single late-in-the-game thirty-yard run when the Saints were up by twenty.

"From the moment I signed with the Saints," Drew said after the game, "I was looking forward to this. It was a great night. It's something we'll never forget."

"It was so emotional on the sidelines," Reggie agreed. "We talked all week about making a difference with special teams. Today we put it to work and made it happen."

Even Falcons coach Mora had to give us a nod.

"Hard as it is to lose this game," he said, "I'd be lying if I didn't say there was a little, little piece of me that really appreciated what this game meant to this city. Unfortunately, we made it way too easy for the Saints."

As the fans walked out of the Dome and into the streets,

they left with a glimmer of possibility. If the Saints could do this, maybe the city could too.

Would we have gotten all this credit if we'd lost the football game? Probably some of it. Surely the commentators would have cut us some slack. The fans too. We could have blamed Katrina, right?

"Whether we would have won that game or not, I think the fans would have still been happy," receiver Joe Horn said. "If we would have lost, I'm sure they would have still been proud of us. They would have still been happy because this organization is still in New Orleans."

But that would not have been enough for the team, Horn said. "We had to win that football game."

Mike Ditka, who'd done his own stint as a Saints head coach, said he noticed something new. "What Sean Payton is doing down there is outstanding," he said the next morning. "This is the beginning of a new era. There's a whole new enthusiasm."

You have no idea how much I was hoping he was right.

"This night belongs to the city, the state of Louisiana and everyone in the Gulf South," I told the media after the game.

We gave the game ball to the people of New Orleans. Native son Avery Johnson accepted on the people's behalf.

Who deserved it more?

17

CINDERELLA SEASON

2006 WAS THE SEASON the Saints and New Orleans proved to the world that neither one of us had given up.

As I rode around the city that fall, I could think of many ways to describe the local conditions. Battered. Devastated. Maddeningly slow to come back. The word I wouldn't use was normal. There were pockets of hope, for sure. But not nearly enough of them. That's why having the Saints back home was so important. In those first eighteen months after Katrina, the team stood out like a beacon.

I've heard people argue that 2006 was the most significant season the Saints have ever had, even more important than the Super Bowl season that would come three years later. These people have a point. It was the year of Drew and Reggie and a new breed of player. It was a year of beating expectations and winning in the face of daunting odds. 2006 was the year the Saints made clear they were staying in New Orleans for the long term.

And suddenly we had some momentum to build on. Three wins and no losses to open the season, we—a team that could barely get on the field the previous year—were leading the NFC South. Amazing! In a city where everything was going slower, costing more and facing setbacks, here were the Saints, back at home and doing better than anyone imagined we would. If 2009 would become a year of jubilation, 2006 was a year of hope.

Everywhere I went after the return to the Dome, people approached me. Almost overnight, I'd gone from the anonymity of the CVS line and Pat O'Brien's to someone people recognized and were happy to see.

"Thank you so much for being here," they said.

"We're so glad you guys are back."

Even when we lost in Week Four—21-18 at Carolina—we could hold our heads up. These players were actually in the game. We gave Jake Delhomme and the Panthers a real fight. Deuce McAllister pulled us ahead in the fourth quarter. It just wasn't quite enough. Carolina answered with two quick touchdowns. We needed more than Brees's eighty-six-yard touchdown pass to Marques Colston, although that was certainly nice.

Yes, we lost the game that day. But we weren't a team of losers. And so it went, game after game.

We beat Tampa Bay, 24-21, on our first trip back to the Superdome after the big night. On a last-second thirty-one-yard kick by John Carney, we slipped past Philadelphia, also at home, 27-24. The Ravens stopped us in the Superdome, but we turned right around and showed Tampa Bay that our previous Buccaneers victory wasn't a fluke—and we beat them in their house this time.

The rough patch came in Weeks Eleven and Twelve. The Steelers beat us in Pittsburgh. The Bengals beat us at home. People began to wonder if our momentum was starting to fade. But after we taught the Falcons a second lesson, this time in Atlanta and then ran past the 49ers in the Dome, even people outside New Orleans were starting to believe.

And a story line was emerging: *Team and City Ravaged by Katrina Shoot to the Top of the NFL.*

What a fairy tale this was turning into! People in New Orleans were pinching themselves.

Early in the season, people seemed genuinely amazed. "These are the Saints," callers were saying incredulously on local talk radio. "How can they keep winning like this?"

"Our biggest test of the regular season came in Week Fourteen. We were facing the Cowboys in Dallas, and interest was high.

When the schedule came out before the season, we drew one Monday night game: against Atlanta in the dramatic reopening of the Superdome. Everything else was a noon or a one p.m. start. That's the kind of schedule you get when league officials and the networks don't think your team will be a factor. Why squander a valuable prime-time audience on an also-ran? But as the season progressed and we kept surprising people, NBC and the NFL called a scheduling audible of their own. The Cowboys-Saints game, they decided, would be moved to Sunday night and given a national prime-time TV audience. At this point in the season, the Chicago Bears were looking dominant. But right behind them in the battle for high play-off seeds were the Cowboys and the Saints.

Still, most of the commentators agreed: We were going to get slammed in Dallas. The Cowboys were the stronger team. They'd had four years of molding by Bill Parcells's firm hand. The post-Katrina Saints might be a nice Cinderella story. But hadn't the Cowboys already clobbered them in the preseason?

"Coach, your team is playing well, very well," one reporter said to Parcells in a pregame conference call, sucking up a little, I thought. "You manhandled the Saints team earlier in the preseason. Do you agree you have many advantages this week?"

I think Bill surprised him. "Whoa! Whoa!" he said. "I think this thing matches up well. I think these teams are even."

Now, I'd spent enough time in the Northeast to know that when someone from New York or New Jersey—as Parcells is—insists a contest is evenly matched, he doesn't believe that at all. He thinks his side has the edge. He's just saying it's even so that when he wins, his victory will be that much sweeter.

"You have to understand the mind-set," I told our players in one of our final meetings before the game. "He doesn't give us much chance. Let's prove him wrong."

There's some background you have to understand here. My second year as an assistant coach in Dallas, Cowboys legend Troy Aikman and I played a round of golf one day against Parcells and Shawn Humphries, the resident pro at the Cowboys Golf Club. As Troy and I pulled further and further ahead, Parcells got madder and madder. He really didn't like it when Troy and I grabbed a six-pack of Coors Light tall boys for the back nine and began gloating just a little. I remember being pleased by the idea of getting under my beloved mentor's skin.

On the Thursday before the Cowboys game, I told our

players that story. And I made a promise to them: If we won Sunday night, we'd toast our victory on the plane ride back to New Orleans with ice-cold cans of Coors Light.

Technically, that's not allowed under NFL rules. No alcohol on the team plane. But this was going to be an exception. I alerted James Nagaoka, our travel director, about my postgame intentions.

"I'll take care of it," he said.

James is absolutely the best at what he does. He'd worked with Mickey in Seattle, and he handles some amazingly complex logistics. When he says he'll take care of something, it gets taken care of.

We played the game and beat the Cowboys handily in front of the Sunday night crowd. The Cowboys opened impressively with a seventy-seven-yard Julius Jones run. But then we just started racking up the touchdowns: a two-yard run by Mike Karney, a three-yard pass to Karney from Brees, a twenty-seven-yard pass from Brees to Jamal Jones. The Cowboys were clearly a good team, but it was one of those games in which things just kept going right for us. We made more plays than they did. In the third quarter Karney caught another touchdown pass, which we followed with a surprise onside kick. Now there was an interesting idea! We stole possession at the forty and scored two plays later when Devery Henderson caught a forty-two-yard pass and crawled into the end zone.

Evenly matched or not, we dominated the game. For me, it was a chance to coach against someone I think so much of and have so much respect for—and win.

Timing matters in a football season. The best time of the week for an NFL coach is from the moment when you win a game until you go to sleep that night. It's not a large window, but that is your time to enjoy the victory. When you wake up the next morning, you're off to the next project. You're grading the tape. You're making corrections. You may have to travel, depending on whether your next game is home or away. But right after winning a game, before you're on to the next one—that's the time a coach has to unwind.

James had obviously been busy. He didn't stop with Coors Light. He also rounded up some Heinekens and some Amstel Lights, and he had all of it icing in buckets when we boarded the plane. There was only one problem: The flight from Dallas to New Orleans was only fifty-five minutes. Was that really enough to properly enjoy all this beer, especially after you subtracted time for takeoff and landing? I didn't think so.

As we prepared to leave DFW, I went up to the cockpit to see the pilots. "Hey," I asked, "is there any way we can make this flight a little longer?"

The pilots looked a little puzzled. "I guess," one of them said.

"See if we can get that done," I said. "If you can stretch it out to maybe an hour twenty, that would be awesome."

"We gotcha," the captain said.

Route adjustments were made. We swung down around El Paso, then swooped slowly around and back east. In an hour and fifteen minutes, we were landing at Louis Armstrong.

We finished the season 10-6, which was good enough to put us in the divisional round of the play-offs. It was only the second time that had happened in New Orleans Saints history. And this was coming the year after Katrina, when people really worried the Saints wouldn't show up at all.

As the second-seeded team, we would face the Philadelphia Eagles, who'd beaten the New York Giants in the wild-card round of the play-offs.

The Saints and the Eagles were well matched, and I'm not just saying that. Together, we had the two best offenses in the league that year. And the game stayed close most of the way. We matched Philadelphia's seventy-five-yard touchdown pass—Jeff Garcia to former Saint Donté Stallworth—with a four-yard Reggie Bush score. And when their running back Brian Westbrook ran for two touchdowns, one a sixty-two-yarder, Deuce McAllister responded with a five-yard touchdown run that kept us in contention. His eleven-yard touchdown reception from Brees won the game, with the defense holding back a couple of fourth-quarter Philadelphia scares. The Saints recorded a franchise play-off record 435 total yards. Deuce alone rang up 143 of them, also a record. He was magnificent that night.

That bought us a ticket to Soldier Field in Chicago for the team's first-ever NFC championship game.

Not only had we had a winning season. Not only had we made it to the play-offs as the second seed. We'd also won there—and now we were one step away from the Super Bowl. A team that was coming off a 3-13 record, a team that wasn't expected to be a factor at all.

After the Philly game, the feeling in New Orleans bordered on shock. It wasn't just happiness or even delirium. It was more like, "Can this really be true?"

And: "How much farther can this possibly go?"

But we had a daunting task ahead.

For dome teams playing in the postseason, the record in cold-weather outdoor stadiums is not very good. Games like the one we played that January against the number-one-seed Chicago Bears in open-air Soldier Field illustrated this vividly.

It was snowing at game time. The temperature was 28 degrees. We committed five turnovers, which killed us. Chicago kicker Robbie Gould made three field goals in the first half. With a two-yard touchdown run by Thomas Jones, the Bears pulled out to a comfortable lead.

Our guys were miserable. The cold, the wind, the snow. The players were either shivering on the sidelines or sweating on the field in their long johns.

We came within striking distance in the third quarter. Brees connected for a thirteen-yard touchdown pass to Marques Colston and an eighty-eight-yarder to Reggie Bush. But we couldn't overcome the field conditions or the turnovers. We lost 39-14, to the environment as much as to the Bears.

Our Cinderella season was over.

We did learn a lesson from that game—an important one that eventually would serve us well: If we were ever going to bring this city to the Super Bowl, we had to find a way to play this NFC championship game at home.

Win more in the regular season. That was the answer. Ten was just a minimum. Get the home-field advantage of a number-one seed.

We needed to be the home team right up to the Super Bowl.

When we got on the plane at O'Hare International Airport, the weather was still miserable. Our flight was delayed. We sat on the tarmac for more than two hours. We got de-iced. We got delayed. We got de-iced again. Finally we took off for New Orleans.

And when we landed at one thirty a.m., fifteen thousand

Saints fans were waiting outside the airport to welcome us home. Fifteen thousand people! At one thirty in the morning! To greet a team after a loss!

"Thank you," people called out as we walked bleary-eyed through the airport to applause from this huge, unexpected crowd.

"Thank you for such a great season," they yelled.

18

FAN BASE

AS I WAS GETTING to know New Orleans, something occurred to me about playing here: What the fans wanted most of all was effort and presence.

Wins were nice. Same as in other cities. Winning made everyone feel better, the team and the fans. But the fact that these players and I had chosen to come here when so much was in doubt—that meant an enormous amount to the people in this region—maybe even more than the final score of some game.

This outlook is a rare act of generosity from fans to a team—all but unknown in the world of professional sports. In Boston or Philly or New York—in almost any other major sports market—the fans can love you passionately, exorbitantly, unreservedly. And they will love you as long as you deliver the victories that make them feel good about themselves and their team. But string together a few losses? Blow a few important plays? Employ a strategy that flops? Even

147

the most enthusiastic boosters will turn on you in a flash. That is just the nature of this business.

My job as a coach—and the players' job as players—is to perform and to achieve victory. We are professionals. We are supposed to have talent. We are paid for our time. And whether it's football, baseball, basketball or NASCAR, all these sports have concrete ways of measuring how we've done. What's your win-loss record? What's your batting average, your free-throw percentage, your pass-completion rate? Do you keep crashing your car into the wall? Fans sometimes will briefly tolerate poor personal performances on teams that are winning. "Sometimes" and "briefly" are the key words here. But if a team isn't winning, do not expect to get very far with pleas of "Honestly, we tried hard."

But in New Orleans, when we lost, it was nothing like the usual fan-on-coach experience. All we got was support and encouragement. Just the fact that we were open for business meant so much at this time.

We were the home team—their team—and we were home now. These people were so generous and warm and understanding—I'd never experienced anything like that before. I didn't quite know how to respond.

And when we won, it was off the charts. After home games, I wanted to shake hands with every spectator who'd been cheering us on. And it wasn't only me. Lots of the players hung around every game accepting congratulations, signing autographs, posing for photos, trading high fives with the fans. The atmosphere in the Dome wasn't like that of a pro team at all. It was more like college players coming over to the student section after a win—and joining the glee club in a rousing rendition of the school's fight song.

We were building a fan base, retail.

Slowly, this direct player-fan contact became a Saints rit-ual. Players would toss their wrist pads into the crowd. I got into the habit of tossing my visor. People just love to collect this stuff, although I'd suggest giving that visor a thorough scrubbing before it goes on anyone else's head. It sounds almost trivial, but truly it was the least we could do after the many ways local people were supporting us.

Naturally, there was more of this with the people in the low-row seats. They were closer. They were easier to reach. But I noticed myself scanning the second-row balcony, which seemed like a mile away. A smile, an acknowledgment, even a nod—I knew how much the personal contact meant.

People got a kick out of Mr. Benson's second-line dance with a jazz-band parasol whenever there was something to celebrate. And now that we were back in the business of win-ning, we were all seeing more of that. After the home games, when our players and coaches were showered and dressed, they would go to a tented area to unwind for an hour with family and friends. Then they would head off to their cars, where they would inevitably be met in the garage by happy fans. That would never happen in security-conscious New York or Washington. In most NFL cities after 9/11, you'd be lucky to catch a glimpse of a player's Mercedes zooming out of the team garage. But it was just taken for granted and enjoyed here.

I'm not saying the fans didn't like the winning. Of course they did. I'm saying there was something as important as success on the field: We cared and we were there.

And then there was the matter of crowd noise.

When you play or coach in the NFL, whether you're at

home or on the road, there's a white noise from the stands that you just become used to. Walking out of the tunnel and hearing the sound of the crowd—you get used to that. Not right away, but eventually. And that white noise, the cheering or the booing—it's like it's all being filtered through big sheets of cotton. It's there, but it gets dulled out. You become accustomed to it, and it's not as moving as it was your first year in the league. You're a professional. It's just the noise.

But it was different in New Orleans. It wasn't a white noise. It was . . . clear. And it started with the region itself, and it wasn't just the sound inside the Dome. The clarity was all-pervasive, on and off the field. It was the lack of artifice in this place, the actual human touch, going all the way down to where the players and coaches lived. In this city, there was far less insulation between the city and the team. The logistics simply didn't allow any insulation. Insulation is not what New Orleans is about.

There are only so many neighborhoods. Uptown, Mid-City, Marigny, the Garden District, Metairie, the West Bank, the Northshore. All of them are areas where people in the organization live, the coaches and the players. New Orleans is not a place where everyone is on a freeway to the suburbs at rush hour. And so the fan base is more hands-on here. You see each other in the Quarter on weekends, or coming and going from restaurants or the mall. There's just more daily interaction, in-season and off-, with the fans of the New Orleans Saints. Not a day goes by as I drive across the causeway that some other driver doesn't give me a thumbs-up, a horn toot or a nod. This is not a city where a player or a coach can easily hide.

And on a personal level, the people here have been extremely welcoming to us. Despite the early misgivings, I am pleased to say, the Payton family has built a very happy life here. We have terrific neighbors. We've made real friends. We've certainly been enjoying restaurants, the ones with the white linen table-cloths and the little neighborhood joints. Like many people here, we talk a lot about food.

Beth stays busy like any mom with two kids and a charming but challenging husband. Meghan and Connor have thrived in the neighborhood parochial school. Meghan, who is heading off to high school, just made the cheerleading squad, even after she broke her arm performing a standing backspring. Connor may be getting tired of hearing, "You look like your dad." But he loves playing soccer at Pelican Park, and he still enjoys our pickup football matches on the Superdome turf after home games. That postgame ritual now includes the children of other Saints players and coaches. Sorry if we're delaying the confetti cleanup by the Dome maintenance crew.

In our time here, we've come to learn and to love many of the local traditions and quirks. We've picked up more than a few of them. You should see me peel a crawfish now. No one sneers, "Midwesterner!" anymore. Meghan and Connor love beignets. The first time they tried crawfish at one of our backyard barbecues, Beth peeled all the little mudbugs and neatly arranged them on a tray like shrimp cocktail. I believe that was a first for the Northshore. I'm now a major oyster fan. Every Friday during the season—home or away games—the Saints order a huge delivery of char-grilled oysters from Drago's for the team. This works out fine since football and oysters are both at their peak in the R-months.

It's always fun seeing players and coaches from all over the country coming here and opening their eyes—and their mouths—to what's so special about this part of the world. I've yet to meet the player who doesn't like French bread dunked in Drago's afterbutter. And I'm comfortable enough now that I don't have to pretend I love the things I don't. Those sticky hot sauce handshakes at the crawfish boil—*ew!* And king cake, which still reminds me of a cinnamon roll with a plastic baby inside!

As newcomers to New Orleans, we marvel at all the exotic accents and rules-be-damned language use. It won't surprise me when Connor starts the R's at the end of all his words. But I hope I never hear Meghan say, "I just made fourteen." Maybe we'll celebrate at Ruth's Chris with a FEE-lay!

You gotta love it!

The only real sour note in our time here has been the Chinese drywall. We didn't know it at the time, but our new house was constructed with that contaminated building material. We aren't alone in this. Thousands of others have been affected. After Katrina, there was a shortage of American-made drywall. Much of the imported stuff went into homes that were being built or renovated in the Gulf Coast region.

We've learned since then that over time—and especially in a humid climate—this drywall emits certain gases that can have disturbing effects. In our case, it's meant our air conditioners kept failing, our microwave kept going nuts, our house alarm didn't function right, our computer hard drives kept crashing—and Beth's silver jewelry turned black. Thank God, she didn't keep that pricey necklace I tried to give her on Valentine's Day!

Many inspections later, we had to move out of the house. After a top-to-bottom renovation, we've just recently moved back in, and we've joined a class-action suit with other families who've been forced from their homes.

It's a post-Katrina irony, I guess. We arrived here after the storm—and we were still displaced. The experience has definitely made me more sympathetic.

Yes, good and bad, we're all in it together. New Orleans is the most intimate city I know. That smaller scale affects everything. People know the players, these fifty-three ambassadors, and the coaches and team staff. I've been hearing this for four years now: "Gosh, Coach, I met Scott Shanle last week, and he was so nice to my dad and mom." And "We had a chance to visit with Pierre Thomas." Every one of these guys. Jahri Evans and Jon Stinchcomb, Will Smith and Hollis Thomas and Mark Simoneau and Roman Harper.

I guess you could say the Saints are a monopoly here. For much of the team's history, the Saints have been the big-time game in town.

Baseball? There is no major-league baseball, although the AAA New Orleans Zephyrs do play on Airline Drive literally in the shadow of the Saints facility. For most of the time, there hasn't been a strong, consistent basketball presence. The Jazz came and went. So did the old New Orleans Buccaneers in the ABA. The Hornets are here now. But that's relatively new. There's no ice hockey. LSU athletics are significant, but that's in Baton Rouge. They have a good alumni network, but that's not something everyone is into. Really, there's one team that is the home team, and that's the New Orleans Saints.

And there was Katrina, which created such horrific challenges for the team and for the city—but also created one surprising opportunity.

Support for the New Orleans Saints never evaporated with the local population. Something quite remarkable happened instead: It broadened. It spread. The circle grew wider. You could see the proof in the team's marketing reports. People were buying tickets from farther-flung zip codes. People were making longer and longer drives to see the games. And the TV ratings reflected this too.

Part of this, I'm convinced, was a natural outgrowth of Katrina. All those Saints fans had been dispersed from New Orleans. The evacuees had to travel light. But they didn't leave their football loyalty behind. They took it with them and helped it spread—through Texas, North Louisiana, Mississippi, Alabama and the Florida panhandle. And some of this was obviously infectious to the people there. It's hard to watch a Saints game with a bunch of Saints fans and not feel part of something real.

The loyal refugees and their converts needed something to cheer about.

So the fan base today is different from the fan base before the levees broke. It stretches across the Gulf South region. We did what we could to build on that. Those first two preseason games—in Shreveport and Jackson—were part of that effort. North Louisiana and Central Mississippi were Saints Country now. This was happening, and it continued to grow.

All of a sudden, the Who Dat Nation was everywhere.

19

DO GOOD

THIS WAS NOT A team of takers. This was a team that understood. We were getting phenomenal support from the people of a troubled community. We'd damn well better be giving support back.

When I got to New Orleans and saw firsthand how Katrina had ravaged the city and its residents, I knew I had to do something to help these brave people rebuild their homes and their lives. Energizing a football team, winning games—that was important. But I also imagined efforts that were more direct. These people had supported the Saints for decades. They were supporting us still. Wasn't it our turn now? We had to get directly into this fight. I vowed to myself from the beginning that this would be more than a media stunt to sell extra tickets or a quest for flattering PR. The proof would be in our actions. Judge us the same way our players are judged on the field: Not by stated intentions. Not by background or pedigree. Only by what our actions demonstrate. I feel genuine pride at the way the whole Saints organization has helped our community through hundreds of projects large and small.

Deuce McAllister hosted a Cocktails for Katrina fund-raiser even before we were back in the Dome. Reggie Bush installed new turf at Tad Gormley Stadium in City Park, where generations of New Orleans high school teams had played and where the Beatles had once performed. Drew Brees just about adopted the Lusher Charter School. The Brees Dream Foundation teamed up with my charitable group to cover athletic-department operating expenses at George Washington Carver High School in the Upper Ninth Ward.

I'm especially proud of Payton's Play It Forward Foundation. From the start, our focus was on improving the lives of children and families across the Gulf Coast region. Much of the credit goes to Beth and to our executive director, Karen Hegner—and to all the thousands of generous people who keep buying tickets to our fund-raisers and clicking on the DONATE button at www.paytonsplayitforward.com. We've partnered with a couple dozen inspiring groups, including Brad Pitt's Make It Right NOLA Foundation and Dr. Phil McGraw's Dr. Phil Foundation and Blaine Kern's Greater New Orleans First Responders Fund.

Those efforts have made a real difference in real people's lives. But it's the person-to-person things that have meant the most to us.

Like our Saturday tradition before every home game.

Working with the Make-A-Wish Foundation and similar groups, we began inviting young patients with serious illnesses to our final pregame walk-throughs on Airline Drive.

This has become enormously popular and brings great joy to these kids. The requests pour in. Nick Karl, the Saints' community-affairs director, has the impossible task of combing through the hundreds of heart-wrenching letters and choosing a special case or two each week.

This isn't a formal program. It doesn't have a budget or any official name. It's just something we started doing—and never stopped. We don't invite the media. It's just a quiet thing we do on Saturdays. The kids and their families seem to appreciate it. It's brought a huge emotional boost to us.

After a behind-the-scenes tour of the training facility, the children and their parents are invited out onto the practice field. When I get a break, I go over and say hello.

"I have a son your age," I might say. Or "My daughter looks a lot like you." I just try to make a personal connection.

As practice is winding down, the players gather in a giant huddle around the child, applauding and welcoming the child to their practice. That scene is amazing to see, all these giant athletes surrounding a tiny child. By this point the parents are usually crying. Then we ask the kid to break the huddle for the team.

If that doesn't move you, nothing will. It's a special experience for all of us.

Then we'll invite that week's child to join us in the Superdome for the game, watch from the sideline, stand with us in victory or defeat and high-five the players in the tunnel as they run off the field.

"Come with me," I told one boy whose story had especially touched us. I brought him into the locker room and gave him that day's game ball. Half the players were teary by the time they got to the showers.

Some of these efforts were coordinated by the Saints organization. But many, the players and coaches did on their own. It wasn't that any single effort can solve the problems of a region. It was that we've been trying to do our part. It created an infectious mind-set that said: "We are lucky. We are grateful. We want to give back."

We are always hearing how selfish and narcissistic professional athletes can be. And sometimes that's true. That only makes what our guys have done that much more extraordinary.

Pierre Thomas, Lance Moore, Usama Young—they're constantly asking, "What can I do?" I don't believe Malcolm Jenkins has ever refused a request. And it hasn't been only the high-profile stars pitching in. Every Tuesday, backup tackle Zach Strief would ask Nick Karl, "What do you have for me to do?"

"It used to be that when we had a request for a player to appear at a local event, I'd be begging people to go," Nick said. "Now I've got ten guys lining up."

Jon Stinchcomb didn't wait for us to organize anything. He made his own relationship at Children's Hospital. He stopped by constantly and has let many of the patients and their families into his life. I know he's been to the funerals of several young people he met there. He's touched them, and they've touched him even more. This is so much more than the average athlete's twenty-minute drop-by to sign some autographs.

Scott Fujita is adopted. He wanted to do something with adopted kids. We partnered him with AdoptNOLA, the adoption-services arm of Catholic Charities Archdiocese of New Orleans. His mom was a two-time breast cancer survivor. Scott wore a pink hat on the sidelines.

People kept asking, "Why's the big guy wearing a pink hat?" That was why.

Several years in a row, Steve Gleason let his hair grow to his shoulders and then cut it off, put it in a Ziploc bag and mailed the hair to a group called Locks of Love, which creates hairpieces for children who've lost their own hair. Somewhere, there are several young cancer patients running around with Steve Gleason's hair.

The giving goes on. I think most of the players would tell you they've gotten as much as they gave.

Many of these players are barely out of college when they come to us. They're twenty-two, twenty-three years old, living in a strange new city where they hardly know anyone. I've seen this happen over and over. By getting involved in the community, they discover that some things in life are more gratifying than sitting on the couch in their off time playing Xbox all day.

"It's much more rewarding to get out and help people," I'll tell anyone who asks. "You'll meet people outside of pro football. You'll be connected to this place you're living in. You'll care about some brand-new people. They'll care about you."

Defensive tackle Anthony Hargrove, who's had some troubles in his life, wanted to help young people who maybe weren't going down such a good path. He found them at the juvenile detention center in New Orleans. He brought Reggie Bush along.

The young inmates were in shackles when the players got there. Their shoelaces had been taken away. Anthony related personally to all of that. He described his own childhood in a Brooklyn tenement, his mother's early death, his time in homeless shelters and foster care and the drug tests that he'd failed. "You are never so far down," he said that day, "that you can't get back up again."

Anthony was proof of that, and those kids heard him. From what I heard, even tough-guy Reggie was moved. He'd been through some stuff, but never Hargrove-level stuff.

Every team in the NFL has some kind of community-relations program. All of them do good works. But I challenge you to find any team where giving back is more central.

It's a fair exchange, I figure. No community has meant more to a team.

One special day still sticks in my mind. On that June morning, we called off our regular practice. Instead of taking the team to play paintball or to a water park, we loaded everyone onto buses and rode into the city's low-lying Hollygrove neighborhood. This is an area that floods in a stiff August rainstorm. After Katrina, Noah's Ark would have fit right in. Some of the local residents were already rebuilding. Ever so slowly, the neighborhood was coming back. But lots of folks were still waiting for their insurance checks and their Road Home funds. Others didn't know what to do. Some were losing hope that assistance would ever arrive.

Again, we didn't turn this into a media event. I just told the players the afternoon before: "We won't be having a regular practice. You may want to wear your jeans."

This was a whole lot more than a ribbon-cutting or a shovel-in-the-earth photo op. The Saints organization made a $50,000 donation to the Hurricane Katrina Fund. And ninety people from the team—players, coaches, office staff, even Mr. Benson—put four New Orleans families back in their homes. Hammering nails. Hanging drywall. Painting

walls. Hauling lumber. Raking debris. Building fences. Plant-
ing trees. You should have seen me with that Weed Wacker.
Those weeds didn't stand a chance. Guys with construction
experience climbed up on scaffoldings and worked with
power tools. These were highly skilled professional football players working as laborers now. Here was Will Smith,
wearing a fiberglass mask as he pulled down drywall. There
was Charles Grant, using a power drill. Everyone did what
they could. As a group, we did pretty much everything that
had to be done to renovate some badly flooded homes. This
was a large, focused crew used to working together. Even in
a day, we made real progress.

I think it's fair to say that no one expected a professional
football team to do something on this scale.

"Within half an hour of getting off the bus, they were all
on the job," marveled Kristin Gisleson Palmer, director of
Rebuilding Together New Orleans, the group that helped to
organize the project. "It wasn't until they were nearly finished that people in the neighborhood knew what was going
on. There wasn't a lot of stopping and gawking. Coach really
wanted his guys to work."

Kristin got that right.

When we were finished, every one of us was dirty and sweaty.
We had blisters and scrapes and bruises. These guys were used
to football practice. But this was real work. And yet there was
an almost giddy feeling of "Look what we just did."

This addressed a tiny fraction of the total need in the New
Orleans area. But it was another step in a long march of
progress, and the results were right there to see. A crew of
ninety people, many of them large, strong men, can accomplish a lot in a hurry when they turn their attention to it.

And you know what made the day totally worthwhile? Spending a little time with the families who were moving back into those homes.

I don't know if eighty-year-old Doris Garrett was a Saints fan before the team showed up that day. After Katrina, she'd been evacuated to Lake Charles, relocated to Georgia and then moved back into a FEMA trailer next to her house in Hollygrove. But I'll bet she's a Saints fan now. Just like retired dockworker Alex Tumblin, who'd been staying in Texas and was thrilled finally to be coming home. And Harry Vanderson, who'd owned his house since 1972 and was evacuated to Gray, Louisiana. And Reedell Parker, who lost his sight in a car accident before Katrina and had been living on relatives' couches since the storm.

They were moving back into houses that they loved, houses we'd helped prepare for them.

Tell me, what could possibly be more satisfying than that?

20

GETTING KENNY

I MET KENNY CHESNEY for the first time in 2001 when I was still with the Giants. He showed up one day at our training camp. Our quarterback Kerry Collins was a real big fan of the country singer. So were several other Giants. Kenny was doing a show at the Pepsi Arena in Albany. The next morning, Jim Fassel said to me: "Sixteen guys missed bed check last night."

"Sixteen guys?"

"Sixteen," Fassel said. The thing was, it was Dan Campbell, Kerry Collins—guys you just wouldn't expect to be missing bed check. I began to put two and two together. It added up to Kenny Chesney.

I saw him play in Dallas and caught a couple of his other shows. He was really on a roll—a couple dozen Top 10 singles, repeat Academy of Country Music Entertainer of the Year awards, the most successful artist in a new breed of down-to-earth singer-songwriters. He and his band were amazing in concert. By the time I got to New Orleans, I was becoming a real Kenny Chesney fan.

The weekend before the 2006 NFL draft, we still needed a place to hold training camp. A group of us—including Beth, Mickey and Mickey's fiancée, Melanie—drove into Cajun country to look at the campus of ULL, the University of Louisiana at Lafayette. That Saturday night, there was a Kenny Chesney show at the Cajundome.

If you said to me, what do you really like to do in the off-season? What are your vices? I'd say my life is really centered around family, vacations, going out to dinner, maybe working out. I'll play some golf. But there are also cold beer and live music. I love that, those two together.

We made the mistake of not really eating a lot on the way over. We checked in to a little Holiday Inn across the street from the Cajundome. We had our tickets and Kenny's road manager, David Farmer, met us at the gate and took us backstage. There's a little vibe room with drinks and a few appetizers, just a place the band could hang out before the show and visit with guests. Very laid-back. Reggae music playing. Carrie Underwood was opening for Kenny. I know we had some beers.

We went out to watch the show in the mosh-pit area in front of the stage. My brother-in-law was with us, and all of us were singing along. After the show, we went back to the vibe room, and I ended up on a beanbag chair. It was a high-energy show, and I was exhausted.

David Farmer told me later that when Kenny finished the show, he'd asked, "Who's that?" and Farmer replied: "Oh, that's the head coach of the Saints."

"Man, they got no chance," Kenny said.

More than a year later, before the 2007 season, we had a preseason game in Week Three in Cincinnati against the Bengals. I learned that Chesney would be doing a show in Cincinnati that Thursday night.

It's not uncommon in preseason to practice or scrimmage with the other team. I talked to Marvin Lewis, the Bengals' head coach, and we made plans. We'd got a couple good practices in, getting ready for Saturday night's game.

I got a call from David Farmer about the idea of those guys coming out to watch us practice.

Why not? Well, one thing led to another and we decided, Why stop there? We cooked up this crazy idea about signing Kenny Chesney to a contract. He would be a wide receiver for the New Orleans Saints. That's what he played in high school. He was number seven.

Now you have to understand this: Kenny's a guy who lifts weights, works out religiously. But he's a size seven shoe. His stature is lean and smaller than we normally see in the NFL. It was not easy to find a place that sells football shoes in his size. We came up with a plan. Friday morning, we called a press conference to announce the signing of a wide receiver. We did it right in Bengals Stadium, in their little pressroom. We set up a locker for him—helmet, jersey, everything.

I asked Joe Vitt what he thought.

The veteran coach was absolutely dead-set against the idea. "This dog-and-pony show," he said. "What are we doing? This is crazy. We're trying to get ready for a season."

But I like Chesney a lot. And Jersey Joe, you know, doesn't know one country artist from another. But every once in a while, I have to tell Joe, "I hear you. But screw it. We're doing this anyway."

So Friday came. Kenny's bus pulled up. He went into the locker room. We got him squared away. And we walked him in his fresh New Orleans Saints jersey into the pressroom.

There were twenty-three reporters in there. Half the room were NFL beat writers. The others were people from the Nashville Network, CMT and other music and entertainment outlets. I don't think they had ever been in the same room together before.

I started off with a long-winded announcement.

"We need to get more experience in the receiver position," I said. "We need some guys who are used to playing in big lights and big stadiums, guys who aren't afraid of the crowds."

People who don't know country music may not understand. What Ali was to boxing, what Michael Jordan was to basketball, that's Kenny Chesney in his world.

I went on. "We need some experience and somebody who's willing to play in a big spot, very comfortable in that role. Now we are in the midst of negotiations because we don't know if we can afford him. And he has some concerns about running pass patterns over the middle."

This was a full-fledged pregame press conference. Backdrop New Orleans Saints, First Bank and Trust. "And without further ado, we want to welcome our new addition to the New Orleans Saints, Kenny Chesney."

He came up. He had his hat on backward. He had his Saints jersey on.

"If we can get the contract done, and he doesn't run me on any slant or post patterns, we'll have a deal," Kenny said. "I just gotta work it into my calendar."

We had some fun with this and headed out to practice. Kenny practiced with us that Friday.

We got out there, did some drills and a walk-through. The whole time, Joe Vitt had this pout on his face. Joe was dying for us to play poorly in this preseason so he could tell me he was right. So Joe was scowling, and Kenny was having a great time. Our players seemed to be enjoying it. Kenny was in all the drills. He was doing exactly what the players were doing. We put in a couple plays for him. We were coaching him up. I have an album from that day with some fabulous pictures. *A Saint for a Day.*

As practice neared the end, we decided we were going to punt the ball to Chesney. If he could catch the punt, we decided, we'd give the players Monday off in New Orleans. We had a Thursday night game scheduled with the Kansas City Chiefs. So it was already a short week. Now, all the players were hoping Kenny would catch the punt. This was the end of training camp. Any extra day off was big.

Here's what I noticed: Regardless of the interest level in his music, all the players' attention was riveted on this punt. Will he catch it? Will he drop the ball? Will Monday be a practice day?

They were paying close attention to Kenny. They were paying close attention to our punter, Steve Weatherford. They wanted to make sure Steve would feed Kenny a nice, clean, easy-to-catch one—nothing too high.

Steve hit the punt. Chesney got underneath it. He caught the thing, and I'm telling you this was one of those moments when eighty-five grown men looked like they had just been let out of school early.

The whole time, Vitt wasn't smiling. The East Coast–Jersey–South Philly guy wasn't charmed by any of it. Maybe if we'd signed Bruce Springsteen.

The next night we played Cincinnati. In the quarters he played, Drew Brees was nearly perfect. We had two scoring drives. I'd seen enough. I pulled him out. "And by the way," I said, "tell Vitt we're working just fuckin' fine right now with our itinerary and Chesney last week. Make sure he knows that."

Joe was on the headset, standing right next to me.

We beat Cincinnati in that preseason game. After Friday's practice, we made an announcement that we were going to put Kenny Chesney on waivers.

"We couldn't come to terms with the contract," I said. "My gut instinct all along was that we weren't gonna be able to afford him. So I think it was better for everyone."

The next week I got a text from Kenny: *Had a great time. Really appreciated hangin' out. You guys were great. You represent that city with so much class. And the next time your punt returner fumbles, I'm here.*

I chuckled. He'd caught the punt. He was right. That following Thursday at Arrowhead Stadium, wouldn't you know it? Here was a punt bouncing off the head of our returner.

We played lights-out in that game. I remember coming into the locker room and sending a text message to Chesney. I said, *Check out* SportsCenter. *The first punt of the game bounced off our returner's head and I thought of you. Maybe you should reconsider your contract demands.*

21

NEXT SEASON

WE GAVE 2006 A proper New Orleans burial.

I'm not kidding.

We gathered up some icons of the biggest accomplishments of the previous year. A few Player of the Week plaques. The trophies for MVP and Coach of the Year. A game ball from the play-off victory against the Eagles. Some other awards and mementos. We took all those happy symbols of the previous season and dumped them into a big wooden casket I'd brought into the weight room on Airline Drive.

At the same time, I had a couple of guys from the Saints' grounds crew dig a rectangular hole, six feet deep, right beside the practice field.

This was the last day of minicamp in June '07. After practice, I had all the players and coaches gather around the hole, which looked like maybe some plumbing work was being done. But this hole was bigger.

The first thing the players heard was a brass funeral march, a slow, doleful version of "Just a Closer Walk with Thee." The first thing they saw was a New Orleans jazz band marching toward them. Walking with the band was a clergyman in full altar vestments. Cliff and Bum and Dan and a couple of others from the equipment and fitness staff were carrying the casket toward the hole.

Had someone died? Kind of. We were holding a fitting send-off for a year much beloved.

The season was great. It was over. We were moving on.

"It was a fine season," the clergyman said once the casket had been lowered into the hole, "a glorious season. Now it has gone off to join its maker, delivered on angel wings to its just reward." He spoke so movingly, you'd have thought a real person was heading home to God.

There is nothing that can't be commemorated with some preaching and a jazz band.

When the clergyman finished speaking, the band kicked the music up several notches, as they do at all jazz funerals. Suddenly, instead of the slow dirges, the musicians were swinging into a rousing rendition of "When the Saints Go Marching In." We had a real second-line party on the practice field.

Good-bye, 2006, New Orleans–style.

We practiced that summer with the same intensity we had the summer before. Hard on Airline Drive, even harder when we got to Millsaps College in Jackson for our late-summer training camp. As the sweaty days wore on, the guys kept asking: "When are we going back to the water park?" The veteran players even began taking bets on what day we would. Two weeks in, when everyone was exhausted, hot and beginning to tune out the coaches—I finally said, "Today." Everyone was definitely ready for a break and a chance to cool down. But I suspected they were just as eager for a rematch in the five-on-five, defense-versus-offense competition on the monster waterslide. I probably should have known better and not encouraged any of this.

Clearly both sides had been studying last year's results. For all I know, they might have been reviewing waterslide game tape at night. Sliding technique had definitely improved. They were whizzing past last year's Sharpie marks. One by one, they were coming down faster and landing farther out. They had built on Scott Fujita's quick-succession technique from the previous competition: Send the three-hundred-pound lineman down first. He'll force out the water. Follow him immediately with a lighter player built for speed.

Just like football: The big guy blocks and the little guy runs.

All that time, we were running out of slide room. The new Sharpie marks were getting closer and closer to the end.

Then here came Scott Fujita. Down the slide, faster and faster. Rocketing into the flume. Zooming past the Sharpie marks right off the end of the slide. Across ten feet of wooden boardwalk. Past a small patch of concrete. And slamming squarely into a very solid fence.

Wham! That must have hurt!

Several players let out giant yelps. They were laughing and clapping and shouting all at once. "Oh, my God!" "Scott!"

At about the same time, a rush of panic was sweeping over me. Our starting strong-side linebacker just went into a water-park fence, and he now was limping.

As he pulled himself off the ground, Scott seemed genuinely conflicted. He didn't want to diminish the fact that he had won so spectacularly, that he was now the back-to-back champion of the water-park games. He pumped his arms in the air. At the same time, he really couldn't walk.

A trainer ran for a bag of ice. He put it on Scott's ankle. Scott hobbled to the bus. And for the next eight days, Saints linebacker Scott Fujita had to wear a boot on his foot and couldn't practice with the team. He missed a preseason game.

You try explaining that to the New Orleans media! Easier than the New York media, I guess. I was just waiting for the sports-page headlines in the *Times-Picayune*: "Not So Funny Now: Coach's Reckless Outing Costs Saints Dearly" or "Water-Park Splash-Back: Under-Manned Defense Drowns." He'd survived two weeks of two-a-days. He went to a water park and was sidelined for eight.

All I can say is thank God we'd won in 2006. Something like that, on the heels of two losing seasons, the head coach would soon be looking for a job.

We opened the season in Indianapolis with a Thursday night lopsided loss to the Super Bowl champion Colts, 41-10. We followed that with three more losses—Tampa Bay, Tennessee and Carolina. This was not nearly as fun as opening 3-0. Deuce McAllister injured his knee in the Tennessee game and would be out for the season. That was a costly injury for the team and the second major knee injury in three years for Deuce.

It didn't take long for some of the football experts to start labeling our team a one-hit wonder. And when a few turned skeptical, others quickly jumped on the bandwagon. Not the real fans. Not the New Orleans people. Certainly not the fifteen thousand who had turned out at the airport to greet us after we'd lost the NFC championship game—they had more patience than any fans I'd ever heard of. "Don't let it rattle you, Coach," a woman in a Saints jersey said to me as I walked out of the Superdome after the Carolina game, our fourth straight defeat. But the national media, even some in the local media, were asking tough questions, which was appropriate, and I really thought we needed to answer them. The pre-Katrina Saints defeatism was beginning to creep into the fan base.

"Yeah, one good season!" I heard a man grumble while standing in line at the Winn-Dixie supermarket. "But they can't win a championship." I'm not sure if he knew it was me who was standing there.

"We need to get a flatbed trailer in here," I told Mickey after loss number four. "And I want enough musical instruments for a five- or six-piece band. Cheap ones. They won't be returning in good shape."

Mickey arranged it.

And so the week before we flew to Seattle to play the Seahawks, a flatbed trailer was parked at the corner of the indoor practice facility. On top of the trailer was a saxophone, a trombone, a trumpet, a drum set, a tuba and a guitar. There was also a metal pipe wrapped with tape like a baseball bat.

I'm not sure what the players thought as they headed out to practice. Maybe that there'd been a function there the night before and the band hadn't returned to collect its instruments.

After practice, we gathered everyone near the trailer and I addressed the team.

"Do you know what a bandwagon is?" I asked the players. I got a few vague answers.

"This is a bandwagon," I said. "The bandwagon goes way

back through the history of street parades. It's a wagon or a trailer or a flatbed truck that carries the band in a parade. The bandwagon is a popular place to be. People like to follow the bandwagon and jump on it, even dance on the bandwagon. Some people do it because they see other people doing it too.

"This is where the music was. But you'll notice," I continued, "this bandwagon is empty now. No one's on it. There's no music being played. That's what happens when you're 0 and 4. No one wants to be on this bandwagon with you."

And then I picked up the metal pipe and I started swinging hard. I beat the hell out of all those instruments. Bent the cymbals. Decimated the drums. That pipe was so heavy, even the trombone and the tuba didn't have a chance. The trumpet or the guitar either. By the time I was finished, there was nothing but a pile of mangled junk on that bandwagon.

"From this point forward," I said, "we're not letting anyone else on this losers' bandwagon. It's time for us to be winners again."

Normally we traveled on Saturdays. But we went to Seattle a day early so everyone could get acclimated to the time-zone change. We had a light practice at Qwest Field that Saturday morning. We changed things up a bit. Instead of the offense running their scripted plays and the defense running theirs, we made everyone on defense play an offensive position, and vice versa. This lightened the mood. It quickly turned into a competitive pickup game, like the football we'd all known as kids.

The following night, we defeated the Seattle Seahawks handily. It was a prime-time game, and we were a heavy underdog. But when you're 0-4, any win's a big win. The next week we beat the Atlanta Falcons. Could the momentum be going our way again?

One other factor might have played a role. Two victories in, Fujita and a couple of other players went out at night and dug up the casket with last year's accomplishments inside. They carried it into the players' locker room.

They put a sign on the casket that read: "We're back."

I guess they'd met a woman in the city who supposedly knew about these things: "That's not good mojo," she said, "burying your success like that."

The mojo woman might have known what she was talking about. In the next two weeks, we beat the San Francisco 49ers and the Jacksonville Jaguars. Instead of 0-4, we were now 4-4. We didn't manage to turn the season totally around. We finished the year 7-9. We didn't make the play-offs. We didn't experience the same improvement Scott Fujita had on the waterslide. But somehow or other, we rescued the season from embarrassment. And given how we'd started, that was an accomplishment right there.

22

NEW STORM

NINE DAYS BEFORE THE start of the 2008 season, we got the first reports from the National Weather Service: A major storm was brewing in the open waters to the south.

Oh, no. Not again!

It had been almost exactly three years since Katrina. The recovery of the Gulf Coast region was still very much a work in progress. No one knew how the battered levees would hold up in the face of another powerful storm. And Hurricane Gustav, as the new storm was soon officially known, was packing strong winds, kicking up heavy water, and heading in the general direction of the Louisiana coast.

No one was ready for another one. The city and the region understandably were on edge. Would it hit here? How bad would it be? Nobody knew. All we could do was wonder: Would the local economy, housing stock and communal psyche survive another big one? These were valid questions

as Gustav was gaining strength. Already, people were top-
ping off their gas tanks and stocking up on bottled water
and Sterno. You could feel the anxiety everywhere. Mean-
while, we had a decision to make.

Our opening game was September 7 against Tampa Bay
in the Superdome. Whatever happened with Gustav—good
or bad—would probably have happened by then. But what
should we do in the meantime? Prepare to play in the Dome?
Practice on Airline Drive? Take the whole team away to some
distant city?

After Katrina, Mickey Loomis, Tom Benson, Rita Benson
LeBlanc and Dennis Lauscha, the team's top executives, had
put together a comprehensive hurricane-evacuation plan.
Clearly, they'd learned some lessons from Katrina.

We had a team meeting on Friday and I said to everyone:
"Here's what I want you to do. Over the next two days, take
care of your families. I want your wife and your children to
come first. Make sure they have a well thought-out evacuation
plan. If there's anything they need, let us know ahead of time.
I'll see you two days from now at the airport, five p.m. sharp.
I'm still hoping we'll play next Sunday in the Superdome. But
we're going to practice in Indianapolis this week."

It turned out the Colts weren't using Lucas Oil Stadium
that week. They were still at training camp in Terre Haute,
Indiana. So, eight hundred and fifteen miles from New
Orleans, with Gustav swirling and the Weather Channel on,
we prepared for the opening game of the 2008 season.

Some people might think of this scenario as a bad distrac-
tion. Maybe it was worrisome for the fans. But it created
a change of scenery for us. It focused everyone's attention.
And, thankfully, Gustav veered west. It dumped some water

around New Orleans and caused some flooding, but it was no repeat of Katrina. We went back to the Superdome and beat the Tampa Bay Buccaneers 24-20.

2008 had its frustrations, but it got us used to life on the road. Our 8-8 record wouldn't be enough to get us into the play-offs. But that comfort on the road would serve us very well at the end of the following year.

For several years, the NFL has been working to popularize American football around the world. As part of that effort, we were asked to play the San Diego Chargers at Wembley Stadium in London in Week Eight. I was disappointed. Not because I don't like London. I do. But this game would count as a home game for us, and I hated to give up the home-team advantage of playing in the Superdome, even for one game. It's a little easier to swallow if it's an away game. You're traveling anyway. But to lose a home game is different.

Talk about cultural diversity. The Who Dats in London! Crawfish and crumpets! The common ground was good beer. And the locals treated us like, well, royalty. Our following was growing stronger and stronger. New Orleans' home team was picking up fans everywhere. Even in England, people were wearing black and gold.

In the end the experience was a pleasure for all of us. Our players loved London. Our team won the game. Rita Benson LeBlanc and Tom and Gayle Benson did an excellent job hosting the team, the employees, and their families. Everyone did their part—our equipment staff, the video people and the training crew. Football-operations chief James Nagaoka, our everything man Jay Romig—those guys were key. Despite my early reservations, events like this one brought us closer together as an organization. We were getting the one-week road routine down pat. Just like on a concert tour, we brought everything. A year and a half later, this very same traveling road show would pack up its act and head to Miami for an even bigger game.

Something else was becoming apparent: how much we depended on our two main football scouts, Rick Reiprish and Ryan Pace. The strength of our roster over the years has benefited tremendously from the work of these two men and their staffs.

Rick is our director of college scouting. His job is to scour the college ranks for potential Saints players. He studies players. He reviews statistics. He interviews coaches at colleges large and small. He attends more bowl games than anyone should ever attend. His Super Bowl every year is the NFL college draft. Rick and his staff guide all our decisions there. Their efforts didn't begin and end with Reggie Bush. They've also brought us Jahri Evans, Marques Colston, Tracy Porter and many other valuable Saints.

Ryan is our pro-scouting director. He and his staff keep an up-to-date go-to list for every position on the field. Ryan knows the free agents. He knows who is about to go on waivers from the other teams. He knows who's doing anything in the Canadian Football League and elsewhere. If a defensive end or offensive guard gets injured in a game on Sunday, by Monday morning Ryan will be telling Mickey and me: "OK, here are our possibilities. Here are the three best players available now. I can fly all three in tonight. We'll work them out tomorrow." And by Tuesday night, that position will be filled. Ryan finds players like Jon Vilma, David Thomas, Garrett Hartley, Mike Bell, Jeff Charleston, Darren Sharper and many other great finds. It's his job to bring them to Mickey and me.

But we still had a season to finish and some lessons to learn. Thank God we had advisers like Joey Imparato.

Joey was a high school classmate of mine, a street kid from Chicago. As teenagers, we'd played poker at his house. His parents were divorced. We all thought his stepfather was in the mob. I have no idea if that was true.

He was just one of these little wise guys, Joey was. If you heard him talk, you'd think he was a little shady. After high school, Joey went on to Las Vegas. I went on to playing and coaching. He worked at a casino for a couple of years, and then he had an accident in Vegas. No one knows the details of it. But he walked with a limp after that and used a cane.

Joey was down in Florida now, married, no kids. But somewhere along this journey, Joey showed back up in my life.

"Tampa Bay," "Coach," "tickets"—classic Imparato. I arranged for him to come to a game. Within twenty minutes, he was talking to a national sportswriter. Then he had a hot dog in the owner's suite. Joey's a guy who, once he's in the building, you can't get rid of him. We all know a guy like Joey.

After that, Joey developed a routine with me. He'd call my cell phone every Thursday with what he thought should be my message for the team before the next game. Joey loves sports. He used to play sports, and he'd been studying coaching for years. One thing Joey has is an ability to get a good read on people.

So every Thursday I would get a voice mail. Often, there would be a second one because the time on the first voice mail had run out.

We'd be on the team plane. I'd say to the guys, "You gotta fuckin' hear Imparato this week." I'd put the speaker on and Mickey, Gregg Williams, Joe Vitt and I would all lean toward my cell phone.

Every time we go on a trip, it's, "Hey, did Joey call?"

"Yeah, wait till you hear it."

We went to Detroit. This was just before Christmas 2008. The Lions hadn't won a game all year. We were 7-7. They were 0-14.

Joey had some thoughts.

"Yo, yo, yo, yo, yo, baby—now pay attention," he said. "This week's fuckin' easy. I'm puttin' this week on coaching. Now listen to me, you guys are way the fuck better than the DEE-troit Lions, but if you go in there and fuckin' fart around for a quarter and a half and lose this game, you'll have a shit-eatin' Christmas. Tell these fuckin' guys they gotta come in and"—Joey delivered one of his better rants.

We were on the plane. It was hilarious. It was awesome. "You'll have a shit-eating Christmas." Who says that?

When we got to the hotel in Detroit, I went to see the banquet manager and asked: "Can you get me a loudspeaker system in the team meeting room so I can hold this phone up to the microphone and have everyone hear it clearly?"

"Yeah, yeah, yeah, no problem."

We had our pregame meeting, and as we were winding down, I said: "Look, some of you haven't met this guy. Some of you may have seen him at a practice. I went to high school with him." I gave them a little rundown of Joey's background—the casino work, the mysterious accident, the weekly phone calls. "He follows us very closely, and every Thursday I get one of these calls. It's his message to you guys."

A few players looked sideways, not quite sure what to make of the concept of getting advice from one of the coach's hometown pals. But they humored me.

I went on. "I listen. I chuckle. Sometimes it's humorous. Sometimes he's right on. Other times, he's way off base. But I want to play this one for you. He's dead-on here. Joey Imparato."

I hit PLAY on the voice mail, and there was Joey's voice.

"If you don't fuckin' get off the fuckin' plane ready to kick some ass, it'll be your worst fuckin' Christmas—you go get their ass. You hear me? You tell these fuckin' guys it's all on the coaches—every one of your fuckin' coaches better get their guys goin'."

The players were just howling at Joey's advice. I'm not sure if it was Joey's language, his accent or the sharpness of his insights. Probably some combination of all three.

But let me tell you, Joey connected that day.

And as Joey would put it, we kicked the shit outta Detroit that week. It was 42-7, fuggedaboutit! I'm not sure how much credit Joey deserves. But his inspirational words certainly didn't hurt.

Of course Joey heard about what I had done. He doesn't miss too much. And it only encouraged him. "Coach, hear me out now," he said the following week, which was the Carolina Panthers at home. "This is a two-part deal here..." And Joey was on to the next game.

Joey was never going away.

23

SEEKING PERFECTION

THERE IS NO SUCH thing as a perfect game, much less a perfect season. Football is a complex human endeavor, encompassing a nearly infinite number of decisions, calls, moves, plays and strokes of luck. There is no way to do everything perfectly. So even if a team wins 50-0, that doesn't mean every player did what he was supposed to. It doesn't mean every play call was right. It doesn't mean there aren't lessons to be learned and improvement to be made.

In football as in life, perfect is an ideal—and remains one.

That said, every game will have a winner and a loser, and the record book counts a win as a win. So as each new season draws near, greatness as defined by a long string of victories is always a genuine hope if not an actual possibility. So it was with the 2009 New Orleans Saints.

And we weren't just dreaming this time.

There are only thirty-two teams in the National Football

League. Each year, two or three of those teams will make a crucial leap from 8-8 into the postseason play. As we moved into the 2009 season, we had two strong reasons for hoping one of those teams would be us.

We felt like our off-season acquisitions were going to help us. We had signed Darren Sharper and Jabari Greer. Jeremy Shockey, Jonathan Vilma and Tracy Porter were going to be healthy. These were key improvements at key positions.

And we hired Gregg Williams. That was huge. We needed someone who could bring a little swagger to the defense, someone who could raise the confidence level a bit, someone who could help us build a truly complementary game.

During our 8-8 '08 season, many people had been saying, "They were first in the NFL in offense. If only they had a defense." The reality was not quite so one-sided. We had failed offensively at Washington to convert a third and short and close that game out. We had failed offensively at Denver to take advantage of field position. We had failed offensively in a handful of games in our ability to run the football. Those failures also hurt our defense.

So it wasn't just the D half of our team that had created disappointment.

Still, while we worked to sharpen our running game, we needed new leadership on defense. I had to fire Gary Gibbs, our defensive coordinator, and that was hard. Gary was the first person I had hired. We'd flown to New Orleans on Mr. Benson's plane and checked in to that seedy hotel where the furniture kept falling apart. Gary was still waiting for that six a.m. wake-up call. Together, he and I had laid down the don't-blame-Katrina rule.

But I was convinced Gregg Williams was the guy.

Gregg had spent the year in Jacksonville, and it hadn't been a good fit for him. I'd never met him before, but I had seen Gregg when he was with the Redskins and I was with the Giants and the Cowboys. He was always tough. He brought real confidence. And people around the league respected him. I would not describe him as wild. But he definitely had an ego. And he was fearless about saying what was on his mind.

Other teams were interested in hiring him—Green Bay and Tennessee and Houston. But he liked the idea of coming to New Orleans with Drew Brees. As defensive coordinator, he knew he would have that support offensively. And we also had a position we could offer his son, who had graduated from Princeton and was working as a coaching assistant in Jacksonville.

But there was a money issue. In our league, $1.5 million for a high-end defensive coordinator is not considered crazy money or way too high. Some might argue it's a pretty good deal for a team. But we had a set budget to work within and not much wiggle room. The offer was $1.25 million.

Mickey and I were having this discussion on a Friday night. I had a few beers in me. I had just signed a new contract for myself. I guess I was feeling flush. "Take $250,000 out of my salary," I told Mickey. "And let's get it to that million-five number. Let's not lose out on this opportunity over $250,000."

I wanted Mickey and Mr. Benson to see the confidence I had in my decision to hire Gregg.

I understand the ownership pressures here. You bring in a new guy. For some period, you're still paying the salary of the guy who left, whose contract still has time on it. So it's easy for me to say, "We want to get this guy"—but there's a lot that goes into it. I just wanted to say, "Hey, I feel strongly about the decision."

Mickey spoke to Mr. Benson and called me back.

"We'll do this," he said. "We'll make the offer."

"That's just for year one," I said, making sure my gesture of confidence didn't run too far out of control. "Not every year. Let's make sure we're on the same page."

When I woke up on Saturday morning, my wife said to me: "You did what?"

Gregg, to his credit, never said anything about the money to me. Not until we were on the field after the Super Bowl, waiting for the trophy to be presented, would he allude to it at all.

"I never brought up the money," he said.

"I know you didn't," I told him.

"I appreciate that," he said.

"I know you did," I said. "Listen, it was worth it."

Enough said.

One other fact made it easier for me to be gracious. At the end of the season, Mr. Benson wrote me a check to cover what I'd pitched in. I think he wanted to do that at the start of the season. I don't think he paid me back just because we were winning. "He just was appreciative that you felt that strongly about the decision," Mickey said.

So Gregg's arrival was a big reason for the optimism. From the start, he was working well with the defensive coaches who were already with us. He meshed well with Joe Vitt. There was a better balance now on the team. The secondary got a face-lift. The leadership had changed. The attitude had changed too.

Yet honestly, before a season ever starts, you don't know how it's going to end up. In '06, I would have told you we were only gonna win three games, and we went to the NFC championship game. And our schedule was a tough one. We had the AFC East—the Patriots, the Dolphins, who had just won their division, the Jets and Buffalo. That's a strong division. And we had the NFC East—Dallas, New York, Philadelphia and Washington. Those were arguably two of the better divisions in our game.

With Williams finally on board, we opened well against Detroit at home, 45-27. Then we went immediately to Philadelphia to play the Eagles. This game was the game that really put us on a roll.

In four years, we had played the Eagles three times—twice by schedule and once in a play-off game. All those games were in the Superdome.

But having coached in Philadelphia, I know something about Eagles fans. This '09 game was maybe my eighteenth time preparing to play in Philadelphia. Andy Reid is excellent. The Eagles are extremely well coached, the most successful team in the NFC over the past ten years. And going into Philadelphia is the antithesis of going to a place like Green Bay with all their bratwurst hospitality. The Philadelphia welcome to a visiting football fan is more like: "We really don't fuckin' want to see you on game day." It's even worse for an away team that has come to Philly for a game.

I warned the players a week before the game.

"This is gonna be a little different for some of you who haven't been to Philadelphia before," I said. "The four buses are gonna come off the highway. We'll do a loop around the stadium. As we come back to the basketball arena and we're getting closer to the Linc [the Lincoln Financial Center], we will pass a group of tailgaters. A large group of tailgaters. A big parking lot. And I promise you, bus number one is getting at least four eggs. Now bus number four, you might get more. But I promise you, bus one's getting four eggs."

I explained a bit of what I had learned while coaching in Philly and playing there over the years. And I'd lived there a few years as a kid. We lived in Newtown, Pennsylvania, from the time I was seven until I was thirteen. Before we moved to Naperville, which I still consider home, we were outside Philly. So I knew something about the history and the local temperament.

"These people are masters at being miserable," I said. "These are the people who boo Santa Claus."

I made a prediction: "It'll start with the eggs being thrown at the buses," I told the team.

"But I'll say this: There's no more gratifying city to win in on the road than Philly. And after we win this game, we're gonna take two laps around the stadium on our buses before we head to the airport because we can't get enough of people pissed off at us and flipping us the bird."

Now, as a coach, there is nothing better than telling your players something is going to happen, and then it happens just like you said. You gain instant credibility with the team.

So sure enough, we pulled around the corner, and here's the parking lot and there are the tailgaters and—*Bam! Bam! Bam! Bam! Bam!* Five eggs.

"Coach! Coach!" the players were shouting.

"What did you think? I was lying to you?" I asked.

Two of the eggs were thrown by what must have been a

nine-year-old boy. And his father was holding the carton. Learned behavior, I believe this is called.

So we pulled around. We went into the stadium. We played a close game in the first two quarters. It was 17-13 at the half. And then we really pulled away. It was a big win for us: 48-22. On the road against Philly! That was a huge win for us.

We're back in the locker room. We gave away the game ball. We showered. We got on the buses. And I told the driver, "Two laps around the stadium."

We only got one.

The motorcade that was taking us to the airport, they were Philly. The police escort, Philly. I told the players, "If you didn't recognize somebody already, if you're not used to seeing them Monday to Friday, they're Philly." And all these Philly people, they take their losses very personally.

They were not about to give us a double chance to gloat.

We took one lap around the stadium. Then it was right out on the highway to the airport.

24

PRESSURE COOKER

THERE IS NO TEAM in this league that can't beat you. You can never forget that.

We arrived in Buffalo after that big win in Philly. It was a game that you would look at on paper and say: "That's a win. We should win that game." And yet traveling to Buffalo is always a challenge. We had a crisis that week that developed and revolved around our defensive line.

We had a player who was late for a meeting—Bobby McCray. On Thursday, I called the team up and really challenged the defensive line. Will Smith, Charles Grant, Bobby McCray and the tackles. I really got after them, the idea that we're not ready for this game. The response was a hard-fought game, but a win in which we played well defensively. I don't know that the Bills had a first down in the second half.

So we were 3-0 with two road wins. Road wins are big in our league. No one was talking about a perfect season yet, but the term "big game" was being thrown around in the media. "This is gonna be a big game!"

Well, if you're going to be a good team, you'll be playing in lots of big games that are bigger than the one that was supposed to be a big game.

Week Four. The Jets in the Superdome. That was a big game. We fought and won another tough game. 4-0. The Giants were next. That was a bigger game. Like us, the Giants were unbeaten.

But we had a bye week before the game.

The bye week was an issue. In previous seasons, we had gone 0-3 in games immediately after a bye week. We just didn't play well coming off a bye week.

That was casting a shadow over our preparation for the Giants game.

There's a tent underneath the Dome where the players, the coaches and their families go to take a deep breath and relax after a game. We were in the tent after we beat the Jets. Everyone was asking how long the players would get off, what the bye schedule would be like. Drew and Brittany were talking to Beth and me.

Drew was lobbying for giving the guys a little more time off. Your instinct as a coach is not to want the players gone so long. But Drew made a good argument.

"Hey," he said, "we haven't played well with our current bye schedule. If we want to do something we've never done before, we've gotta do things we've never done before."

I liked that. "If we want to do something we've never done before, we've gotta do things we've never done before." That could apply to a lot of things around here.

Of course the wives both agreed with Drew. Three to one,

I'm outnumbered here. Drew had a good pulse for where the players were.

We brought the players in for a day after the game and then got 'em outta there for four or five days straight. Took the rest of the week off. Normally, we would have brought them back on Wednesday. We didn't get them back until the weekend.

We had a couple good practices on the weekend. Monday, we got a bonus day in.

Tuesday the players were off—normal routine—and here we got into our game week schedule.

Getting this rhythm right was important. The issue would come up again, twice in the postseason, at the start of the play-offs and before the Super Bowl. Both times, we had a weekend off. We couldn't let that stall our momentum.

We played very well against the Giants. We did two things we had never done before: We changed the rhythm, and we won. That win gave us instant credibility because the Giants were perceived by many at that point in the season as the team to beat in the NFC.

They struggled later. But we beat a 4-0 team, beat them convincingly. And the way we won the game was significant. Gregg Williams was making a difference. We kept turning the ball over defensively. We were leading the league in team takeaways. Some people had been asking, "Is this just a fluke? Are the Saints as good as their record?" That was answered with that Giants win.

There wasn't talk of a perfect season. Not yet. Not at 5-0. The talk was "You're one of the players now in the NFC." There was Philly. There were the Vikings, who were playing well at that point. There was a handful of teams being discussed. We were one of the four or five.

Week Seven was a road game in Miami. We were playing last year's AFC East champion at home. They were well
coached by Tony Sparano. We'd spent three years together in
Dallas. It's Parcells, and it's a physical team. We fell behind
immediately. Late in the second quarter, we were down 24-3.
It was not a promising start, and it really was unexpected.
Up to that point in the season, we had barely been behind
at all. We hadn't played from a deficit. We beat the Giants,
and up until that point we'd been ahead in every game we'd
played. Every one.

A play got reviewed and gave us the ball inside Miami's
one-yard line with just a few seconds left in the half. We
were going to kick a field goal. But because of the challenge,
there was a delay, and we didn't score, so were gonna kick
the field goal.

Drew says to me: "If we sneak it, Coach, I can get in."

We were on the one-inch line. We had just enough time for
him to convince me that we could run a quarterback sneak.
If it worked, we'd cut their lead to fourteen points before
the half.

Prior to the play, I ran down the sideline and told the line
judge, "Hey, we're gonna run a quarterback sneak. Make
sure you see this ball cross the plane because he's gonna
cross the plane."

Then I ran back to the bench area, because you're not supposed to be down the line like that. And sure enough, Brees
took the snap and extended the ball over and back, and it's
a touchdown. It was the right call.

We came back in the second half. We gained momentum.
Sharper got an interception for a touchdown. We ended up
winning that game. As poorly as we played in the first half,

I don't know that anyone felt we were out of it. But that was a key step in this unbeaten season: We found a way to win even when we didn't play so well. We ended up winning 46-34. We got to 6-0. That was big.

The wins kept coming. We played a Monday night game at home against Atlanta. We had three interceptions and won 35-27.

Week Nine, we had Carolina at home and fell behind again. It was 14-0, and we were able to come back. At 8-0, people started noticing we hadn't lost a game. At that point, we started battling not just our opponents but this whole idea of a season without a loss. Everyone started drawing attention to our record. And that can be a problem.

Perfect season? You never want your players to be reading these articles in the paper and hearing these discussions on TV.

You don't want to ever lose sight of the process of Wednesday, Thursday and Friday. That's the secret here: What we do on Wednesday, Thursday and Friday. How we practice. How we compete. How we win. You don't want anything—certainly not some hype in the media about how unbeatable you are—interfering with that.

When you listen to Patriots players talk about finishing the 2007 season 16-0, they'll tell you: That last stretch of five or six weeks was a killer. Now you aren't just worrying about this week's opponent. You have the record hanging over your head. That can seep unintentionally into the locker room.

Thankfully, our team had good veteran leadership. They were committed to not letting that happen. So we beat Atlanta and Carolina, victories that got us closer to winning the division, our first goal.

As the season wore on, people were saying, "Well, they aren't winning the same way they won earlier in the year." St. Louis on the road was a hard-fought game. But if you paid close attention, Buffalo was a hard-fought win too—a close game in the third quarter. Miami was tough. The Atlanta game was close at home. The Carolina game, we were down by fourteen. St. Louis was a close game, and finished with them missing a Hail Mary to beat us.

Away games are an extra challenge. We'd won a handful, but that's just not the nature of our game. Tampa Bay at Tampa, we won pretty convincingly, and that was a road game. So we moved to 10-0, and clearly, this unbeaten season now was being discussed—or at least the idea of remaining perfect.

To the media, we did everything we could to downplay that. "We've gotta prepare for the next game. That's all we're thinking about."

Internally, the idea of a perfect season was discussed with the doors closed. "Just understand how we got to this point."

There had been an important meeting early in the year that became relevant. Normally, we would put up the schedule for the players at the beginning of the season—the first four weeks—and talk about finding a way to handle the first quarter of the season. We'd hope to come out of it at least 3-1.

If you keep that pace going, you'll finish 12-4.

But I remembered Brees and a few of the other captains saying, "Coach, when you put up the first quarter, let's not concede any game. Let's just look at the opponent."

"All right," I said. "I hear what you're saying. We're just gonna look at Detroit. Here's the first four games, but Detroit is what we're focused on. We're not gonna talk about how we've got to win three of four here. It's not like baseball, where a manager might say we've got to find a way to split here and then win the next two."

And so after the first quarter of the season, it was 4-0. After the second quarter, it was 8-0. And into the third quarter, Tampa and New England were coming up.

Tampa Bay was a good win. But like the Giants game, New England was one of those incremental hurdles that turn up through the season that can validate your standing as the best in the NFC or a contender to win a championship. Coming back against Miami was important for our team. But New England was in a big spot. A good team with arguably one of the best quarterbacks in football. In that spot on Monday night, we played well again. Against a coach I truly admired.

25

CHANNELING BILL

FROM THE TIME WE got here in 2006, we had closely studied the success of the New England Patriots. That's not so hard to understand. If you were taking over a failing business, you would want to look closely at the practices of the successful companies in the same industry, especially those competitors who were at the top.

New England was clearly a team we could learn some lessons from. In Tom Brady, they had one of the top quarterbacks, maybe *the* top quarterback. They had Bill Belichick as their coach, who is certainly at the top of our game. So we paid a lot of attention to Patriots personnel decisions and how they built a team with character. "What's their recipe?" I was constantly asking myself. "How are they doing what they do so well?"

I had never really spent much time with Belichick until the Pro Bowl in early '07. The coaching staff whose team loses the NFC championship game coaches at the Pro Bowl against the coaching staff whose team lost the AFC game. That would be my crew and Belichick's. We had lost to the Bears. They had lost to the Colts.

Bill and his staff had a tremendous amount to teach a young, first-year head coach. I asked questions: "How would you handle that?" I got their impressions of people in the league. Over five or six days, we just spent some comfortable time together. Bill and I laughed about stuff. Beth and I had Meghan and Connor with us in the hotel, and our suite being directly above his, I cringed at the thought of Meghan and Connor bouncing off the beds and rarin' to go while Bill was reviewing game tape or trying to sleep in. I told him I wished he was in 332-33 and we were in 232-33. We chartered three fishing boats one afternoon and the Patriots' coaches and the Saints' coaches went out deep-sea fishing. Just being able to have a Corona and talk with a guy like Belichick, that was invaluable to me.

It also gave me a chance to develop my Bill Belichick impression. Let me tell you, I do a great Belichick.

So yes, in our industry, this is a guy you would want to study closely. And all of a sudden, three years later, we're playing his team in a big Monday night game—a significant game for more than just the record.

More than just a win or a loss, it was really a game of credibility in our unbeaten season at that point. We were 10-0 when we played the Patriots. And yet the experts were saying, "Well, we'll see how good they are this weekend." We had a few players on our team at this point from New England's roster. Randall Gay and Heath Evans, we acquired as free agents. We traded for David Thomas. Some of these key pieces to our roster were players who had experienced the teamwork, the work ethic, the winning culture, the whole Belichick package of the New England Patriots.

They had a good feel for how Bill Belichick coached. I remember asking Randall, "How would he handle this?" And we'd spent time with Bill, and now we were getting ready to play against him.

I knew I could go into the team meeting on Wednesday and point out to the players some of the things we could improve on to win. But rather than me doing that, why not have Bill Belichick come visit our team?

Why not give our team the chance to hear what Bill Belichick would be telling the Patriots that very morning? I could stand up there and criticize our team. But would the message be clearer if the other coach pointed out our flaws to us?

He's the one on Monday night who would be obsessively trying to exploit them.

OK, maybe he wouldn't agree to do that, to speak to the opposing team before a big game.

But I could certainly do it for him.

I spent some time with Randall, Heath and Dave. We talked about how Belichick would look at us. I watched some tape of Belichick interviews. I made a careful note of how he scrunched up his face and how he tilted his head. I *became* Bill Belichick. The hair greased over to the side and darkened. The blue hoodie with the New England Patriots logo. The khakis and the tennis shoes.

To get the voice right, I went on NFL.com Tuesday night and listened to Mike Lombardi interviewing Bill. Listened three or four times until I had that flat, tightly wound, slightly psycho-sounding monotone exactly right.

And we made a little film.

It was me as Bill Belichick, speaking to the Patriots about all the things that sucked about the New Orleans Saints. Cutting away to video of every imaginable Saints screwup.

Speaking in that trademark Belichick monotone, I opened up indicting myself.

"Tell you what, guys—it's one thing about this New Orleans Saints team. This head coach, wherever he's been, they've turned the ball over. They've turned it over in the Pro Bowl in '06, when I was with him. They don't take care of the ball."

As I—or Belichick—spoke, the B roll featured some of the Saints' worst fumbles, most of them committed by guys sitting right there in the room.

"The quarterback's undersized. We're gonna be able to knock down passes inside. We gotta push from the pocket."

There was Drew being creamed. And on it went.

"The tight end—hell, we traded the tight end, Dave Thomas. He can't block at the point of attack. The halfback, Reggie Bush, is afraid of contact. The wide receivers are guys you have to jam at the line of scrimmage. This Gregg Williams, their defensive coordinator, he gets caught up in all these fancy schemes. And fundamentally they don't tackle very well."

And I went on like that, basically pointing out all these truths about our team. But it wasn't me saying it. It was Bill. And it wasn't just the players Bill was ripping. It was me. It was the defensive coordinator, the offensive line coach. We were all getting criticized.

These are the things that are said when the doors are closed. These are things your opponent says about you.

"These fuckin' corners, they're small. We can go make plays. Randy, this is easy. Tommy, this is a lights-out game for you."

As I was playing the tape for our players, you know that Bill was talking to his team in Foxborough, hitting exactly all those keys.

I went on like that for a full forty minutes.

When you do something like this, you step out of the norm. You deliver a message that will connect with the team in a much deeper and more profound way.

It doesn't always work. As a coach, sometimes you swing, and maybe you hit a foul ball or you miss. You step away from the plate, and you say, "I don't know what I was thinking, but that wasn't it."

Then sometimes you make solid contact. And every once in a while, you just hit one right out of the park. That's the truth. And this was one of those. Hit it right out of the park!

There were a few muffled laughs in the room right at the beginning. But then the video came up of us fumbling the ball. The video came up of us missing tackles. The video came up of us getting a field goal blocked. The video came up of us getting beat deep. And the video was hitting on each of these points. There were six batted-down balls from Brees. There were the turnovers, the tackling, all the things that as a coach you want to talk to your team about. And we put it together, and it was right up on the screen and Belichick talking to the Patriots team about us.

The humor lasted maybe thirty seconds. Then the room was quiet. Dead quiet.

Because truly, we were being criticized here in a round-about way—myself included. I was the first one. *"The guy hasn't taken care of the football since he was hired in '06. He didn't do it at the Pro Bowl the week I was with him there. That's coaching."*

Message delivered, I would say.

When we left that meeting, of course there were three people I wanted to see right away. I wanted to see Randall, Heath and Dave.

"How close was it?" I asked Randall Gay first.

"I got goose bumps," he said. "I felt like he was sitting in the Patriot team meeting."

The others agreed.

There's an old saying: "Imitation is the sincerest form of flattery." I believe that to be true.

We wanted to be like the New England Patriots. We wanted that. No team has done it better. Coaching, quarterback, defense, teamwork—that was the team. They were the champions as far as I was concerned. And on *Monday Night Football*, the Saints are coming into the Superdome 10-0. People are saying our victories have been lucky. We're not as good as our record says. Our credibility is on the line. This is who we've been modeling ourselves after. This is who we've been talking about. And some of those things Belichick or I or whoever was saying—some of those things were true. Hell, all of them were true.

We still beat his team. Solidly. It was 38-17. They were ahead in the first quarter, 7-3. But we scored another twenty-one points before the half, and the Patriots never recovered. Our defense did a great job. Brees played as well as a quarterback could play. He had a perfect passer rating, which is unheard of in a game like that. By the end of the night, we were 11-0, and something ominous was setting in.

People were looking ahead at the schedule and saying, "Washington, Atlanta, Dallas. If they can get past Dallas, the Saints really could finish 16-0."

I hate that kind of talk.

26

CRISIS TIME

WINNING BEATS LOSING ANY day. We had a couple wins left in us.

We ended up in a dogfight with the Redskins. We had to make some big plays to come back. They missed a field goal late to give us a chance to send the game into overtime. We won a game we very easily could have lost, maybe even should have lost. And yet we found a way to win it. That was twelve.

We went back to Atlanta and had a close game there. We ran a fake punt. It didn't work. Nonetheless, we were able to escape with a win against the Falcons, 26-23. Critics would say we won ugly. OK. But you take the ugly ones too.

We were tired. Mentally and physically. The pressure was building. The expectations were high. We had played that Monday night game against New England, traveled to D.C. in a short week, got their best shot, traveled to Atlanta, got their best shot. And although we won, we won two close games to get to thirteen wins.

The good news was that in Washington we had secured the NFC South championship. But a real issue was being raised: Do you rest your players? Or do you play for a perfect season? Rest and lose momentum? Or do you risk injury to finish unbeaten? It's the risk of injury versus the achievement of finishing unbeaten. That's really it.

The Colts at this point were also unbeaten. Bill Polian was wrestling with the same issue. Minnesota was on our heels a game behind. I talked to our players directly about this: "You guys are gonna hear a lot about whether we're gonna play these last three games to win if we've already got the seeding locked up—or whether we're gonna rest our starters. No one person is gonna make that decision. But our plan—Mickey Loomis, Sean Payton, the coaching staff, the team—we are gonna play to win 'em all."

Clearly, the fans wanted us to play for perfection. The media too. But remember, what's most important is winning the Super Bowl. That being said, we were gonna try to win them all.

And then we lost to Dallas in a big game on a Saturday night. This really was a big game. I made a mistake. DeMarcus Ware, their talented defensive end, was hurt all week. It was a neck injury. You know how serious those can be. All week, the talk was that he wasn't going to play. From a protection standpoint, we didn't pay as much attention as we should have in the event that he did play. Well, he did play. And we—beginning with me—didn't have an adequate plan from a coaching standpoint for helping Jermon Bushrod.

There were several reasons we lost the game. That was

part of it. So was the perfect-season talk. Tony Dungy, the NBC commentator and retired Indianapolis coach, came out two days before that game and said the Cowboys had no chance. I just cringed when I heard him say that.

Dallas was a good team, a very good team. One of the best teams we played last year. They were very good defensively. But they were backed into a corner. It was the month of December. They had not exorcised their demons. No one gave them a chance on the road in New Orleans. It was the prefect spot for them. It was a tough spot for us, and we didn't handle it well. We didn't coach as well as we needed to, beginning with me. The score was 24-17, and I don't know that the game was that close.

No more perfection. We were 13-1.

We were still playing for the one seed. Minnesota lost that weekend. So we still had that one-game lead. We didn't have the one seed sewn up. But we were playing Tampa Bay at home, and surely we could beat Tampa Bay.

There had been a lot of pressure in the past three weeks: "Coach, you guys haven't played as well as you did earlier in the season. And you lost to Dallas. Do you feel like you guys aren't doing the same things you did earlier in the year?"—all that BS.

We went up 17-0 and played a great first half against Tampa Bay. We played well offensively and defensively, did all the things that had gotten us to 13-1. In the second half, it was the opposite. Credit Tampa Bay. They had a big punt return for a touchdown. We drove the length of the field late but missed a field goal. In overtime we couldn't get the ball back or get them stopped in time. You could point to a number of things. Here's loss number two. And here's crisis.

Dallas hadn't represented crisis. Dallas was another good team. The loss to Tampa represented the crisis that you'll face in any season and ours came in Week Sixteen. Crisis. We lost to Tampa Bay. After we lost to Tampa Bay, the Minnesota Vikings lost to the Chicago Bears, which guaranteed us the one seed. So although we had lost the last two games, the New Orleans Saints had secured the one seed that weekend.

So how would we play Carolina? I had made the comment that we were going to play this game to win, and we needed to get back to basics. We needed to get back on the field and do all these things. And when the Bears beat the Vikings—this was important. That changed things. We had the one seed. We no longer had a perfect season to protect. We were going to rest our players.

There was all this talk that no team had ever lost the last three games of the regular season and won a Super Bowl. But you had to weigh this. Did we rest our players, win or lose at Carolina, then get ourselves refocused in the bye week and ready for the play-offs? Or did we say, "Full speed ahead and lose another one"? Now, think about that. Did we say, "We're not gonna take another torpedo here. We took two—Dallas and Tampa. We're not gonna take a third"? Or did we play to win, risk injury—and possibly lose? Now you've taken a third torpedo to the confidence.

So we rested.

Lots of the national commentators thought we had to play this game to win. They said we needed it to get our momentum back. Absolutely wrong. That was one of the best decisions we made all season: to rest our starters in that game. It was absolutely foolish to think that we had to play that game. Who says so? We had the one seed already.

I walked into the TV production meetings for that game. Brian Billick and the guys at FOX Sports were somewhat disappointed. Naturally, if you're the broadcast crew for that game, you don't want to have to look through your flip card to see who's in the lineup. Well, tough. I couldn't give a rat's ass about the interest level you and everyone else have in this game. It means nothing to me or our team.

The production meeting was short. They were disappointed. They didn't ask to speak with any players after they spoke with me.

We lost the Carolina game. Now it's us versus everyone. We've got a crisis here, although the third torpedo wasn't a direct hit. We'd rested our starters. But no team had ever finished 0-3 at the end of the season and then won a Super Bowl.

Listen, we can find a statistic in the rich history of forty-three years of Super Bowl football to show anything. Every year, no one's done this. That being said, we needed to get healthy. We needed to rest. We needed to get ready for who-ever we were gonna play next.

That Carolina decision was tough. But it was absolutely the right decision. Peter King of *Sports Illustrated* was getting ready to kill us for resting our players. It was the last Thursday before the game, and I said to Peter, "Let me ask you this. All right, I'm gonna play all our starters, and we're gonna go full-bent—what if we get our ass beat?"

It was quiet on the phone.

"I never looked at it that way," he said.

Well, you have to.

27

WE'RE BACK

COMING INTO THE PLAY-OFFS, the pressure on us was immense. The shadow of three straight losses. The idea that we'd run out of gas. The notion that, maybe, we had never been as good as our record made people believe. You didn't hear much of that talk from the local fans. They were thrilled we'd gotten this far. As I walked around downtown, there was almost a giddiness in the air. Despite the late-season fall-off, people were still coming up and saying: "You're doing us proud!"

But skepticism was a drumbeat in the national media and from some of the other teams. We certainly understood this was crisis time.

Lose to the Arizona Cardinals, we'd have had a thirteen-win season and still failed to win a play-off game. If we won, though, we'd be right back in the running for a championship.

Somehow, we had to get our old swagger back.

Deuce McAllister was already scheduled to speak to the team on Friday. He was coming to the hotel and was going to part of our pregame buildup. Deuce had played very well three years ago in that game against Philadelphia. We were hoping he might have something inspirational to say.

At midweek, we had to put defensive tackle Rodney Leisle on injured reserve. That gave Mickey an idea.

"Why don't we sign Deuce to the active roster?"

Deuce hadn't played a game since the end of the 2008 season. He'd put on quite a few pounds, and his knees were shot. He'd had some financial knocks with a Nissan dealership he owned in Mississippi. But number 26 was still the team's all-time leading rusher. He'd scored more touchdowns than any other Saint. And he was still beloved by other players and the fans. Who cared if he couldn't run a wind sprint?

"It's a brilliant idea," I told Mickey. "I can't think of a reason why we wouldn't do it."

Deuce wouldn't actually play. He'd be listed as inactive for the game. But we would sign him to the roster. He'd get paid. And he would be an official member of the team. With Leisle out, we had the spot now.

I got Deuce on the phone.

"Do you want the good news or the bad news?" I asked him.

"Give me the good news," he said.

"The good news is we're gonna sign you to the roster. I still want you to speak to the team, but we're gonna sign you to the roster."

Deuce seemed genuinely touched. "Great," he said when I explained what we were thinking. He wouldn't just run with the team through the tunnel as an ex-Saint. He wouldn't be an ex-Saint at all. He would be a Saint, on the roster for the game. Then he asked, a little tentatively: "What's the bad news?"

"Well, you're twenty-six pounds overweight, and I gotta fine you, and that's gonna cost you more than you'll make for the play-off game."

Deuce thought that was hilarious.

I broke the news to the team matter-of-factly. Every team meeting starts with an order of business. I might say, "Hey, we signed such-and-such. We waived so-and-so. And I fined the following players." It's just business, and then we get into the focus of the meeting. I got that from Parcells. It ensures that nothing goes unmentioned.

That morning, I said: "Rodney Leisle was placed on IR, and we signed Deuce McAllister, running back, Ole Miss, to the active roster."

After a moment of "Huh? What? What did he say?" the players realized they'd heard correctly. An instant buzz swept across the room. These guys loved Deuce, and they knew immediately how fired up the fans would be.

A Deuce highlights video came up, some of his great moments set to music. The video culminated in that divisional game in 2006. He was magnificent against Philadelphia.

"Deuce McAllister has always embodied the spirit of the New Orleans Saints and the city of New Orleans," I told the media. "We're excited to have him back with the team and to have him lead us out onto the field."

Clearly, the other players were thrilled. "Deuce deserves to be here," Pierre Thomas agreed, echoing what I am certain was the view of every player and every fan. "He deserves to be in this battle."

As word spread around the city, people seemed truly thrilled, although some fans read even more into the gesture than Mickey and I—or Deuce—had in mind.

As I drove home on Friday night, talk radio was buzzing with callers who thought we were really going to put Deuce in the game.

"Yeah, they're gonna use him in short yardage. . . . Deuce was always great at the goal line. . . .You watch. They're gonna have a package for Deuce."

"Whoa! Whoa! Whoa!" I was saying to myself as I zoomed across the causeway.

As the one seed, we got a bye for the first week of the play-offs, the equivalent of a guaranteed first-round victory. I'm not complaining about that. But being off for a week, while most of the other teams were playing, brought up some other issues. I knew that how we handled the rhythm of that would set a tone for everything that followed.

I'm always looking for fresh models of success. So, of course, I remembered how we had treated the bye week before the Giants game. Instead of using the time to squeeze extra practices out of the players—a coach's natural crunch-time instinct—I was convinced that Drew's advice had been right. At that point, push-'em-hard-in-the-bye-week had an 0-3 record. Let-'em-relax was 1-0.

We brought the players in Monday after the Carolina loss. We had a light practice, then gave them Tuesday, Wednesday and Thursday off, just like we had in the bye week before the Giants game. Everyone was back for half-day practices on Saturday and Sunday morning, and we spent the afternoons learning who the next-round matchups would be.

We were tired. We needed a break. That's not an excuse.

It's just where we were after the New England win, the short week at Washington, Atlanta, Dallas.

It was us and the Cardinals in the day game on Saturday. We had some concern about their left corner, Dominique Rogers-Cromartie. A second-year player out of Tennessee State, he has amazing ball skills. With Kurt Warner, their passing game was a threat. His play-off numbers were staggering.

Given all the pressure and the do-or-die stakes, we had to be aggressive, more aggressive than the other team. Three years before, we had given every one of our players a wooden baseball bat before a particularly tough game. We brought the bats out periodically as a point of emphasis. We decided to do it again for Arizona. So after the Deuce announcement on Friday, I handed a baseball bat to every player in the locker room. I knew that taking those bats into the game—figuratively speaking—would make a far bigger impact than another speech from me about the importance of playing hard.

I didn't know how literally Reggie Bush would take the whole wood idea.

The night before the game, at the hotel, seemed like the right time to reinforce some important parts of the message we'd been preaching all year. We made a video featuring all four of the speakers we'd had during training camp: Jon Gruden, Avery Johnson, Ronnie Lott and Bill Mallory. It was like an inspirational greatest hits.

It was a highlights video. But in the background, you could hear the audio of the training camp talks. It was dark, and there was the voice of Ronnie Lott. You could hear Bill Mallory. You could hear Avery Johnson. The last segment was my old coaching friend Jon Gruden. "One season. One season of your life. One run." The video ended. The lights came on. And there was Gruden, standing at the front of the room.

He spoke directly about how far the Saints had come. "We're in this position now," he said. "You've gotten yourself here. Go finish this thing."

Gruden works for ESPN now. It might have seemed a little strange to have a TV commentator addressing one team. He covers thirty-two teams. We didn't want to make it a big media thing. My thought was "Let's just keep it in-house." That being said, Jon hired me into the league. There was a personal tie there. I had worked for him. I felt comfortable with the idea, and so did he. This was Friday night, and the feeling was no different from how I'm sure it was at the Cardinals' hotel. "We are ready."

Reggie Bush was a big reason for our success offensively. He's a player of enormous dimension. He's certainly been a great asset on punt returns. But I had felt, as the 2009 season wore on, that Reggie needed to run with more power. We spoke about that during the bye week. The message seemed to have connected with him. As he ran onto the field before the Cardinals game, Reggie looked a little scary with that bat in his hand. He was gripping it as he and Deuce led the team out of the tunnel and onto the field. The instant Deuce was visible from the stands, the Superdome erupted the same way it had been erupting since he arrived as a rookie in 2001.

"Deuce! Deuce! Deuce!"

Reggie was pacing around near the bench, still holding that bat, looking like— Well, let's just say I didn't want to stand too close to Reggie that night. Right before kickoff, I had to remind him: "Reggie, no baseball bats on the field."

And then, on the very first play from the line of scrimmage, Arizona running back Tim Hightower ran seventy yards right through our line for a touchdown. That was the turd in the punch bowl.

Oh, no! You gotta be kidding me!

It was John Gilliam in reverse. Cardinals coach Ken Whisenhunt must have been thinking: "Wow, this is easy!"

Truly, everything could have collapsed. All we'd been working toward could have evaporated. With that one deflating play, our confidence and our focus very well could have collapsed.

Could have. But didn't.

Back in the middle of the season, I told Reggie, "You've gotta have balance here. There will be games you don't have as many touches. But we need to keep you healthy throughout the season. Then, on the big stage in postseason, you will shine."

Reggie shined that night: 217 all-purpose yards. A punt return for a touchdown. A fabulous run to score a touchdown. Brees threw the ball a lot. Cromartie—the guy we were most worried about—got hurt in the first quarter. After that, we started throwing probably 80 percent of the time. The matchups were in our favor.

All our players performed like we had practiced. They did what they had learned to do. They looked inside themselves, and they saw winners there.

Will Smith played well. Brees played well. The defense was sharp. Reggie was not only back—he was dynamic. He was the difference in that game. He had the kind of game he got famous for in 2006, finishing with eighty-four yards on five rushes and twenty-four yards on four receptions plus 109 yards on three punt returns. We won convincingly, 45-14.

And what a world of difference that made. Suddenly, everything brightened up. The streak of defeat—three games and one play—had been broken. The crisis was behind us. The monkey was off our back.

28

NEW HEIGHTS

THE DAY BEFORE THE NFC championship game against the Minnesota Vikings, I could tell I was getting the flu.

My nose was running. I had the chills. I was feeling even crankier than I usually do the day before a game. Saturday afternoon was downtime for the players and the coaches, a final chance to relax with the family before the game. I had promised Connor I would take him out to play paintball. He was wanting some father-son time. I was feeling achy when I got home from the morning meetings. But there was no way I was canceling our plans.

Connor and I went out to Paintball Command, my first time since Gleason had nailed me there. My father-in-law, Tom Shuey, came along. We ran around in the woods and got some shooting in. Connor seemed to have fun. But with the paint-gun noise, now I had a headache too. When we got back home, I climbed under the covers and just lay in bed for an hour or so. Then I got up, dressed, had some soup, took some medicine and drove across the causeway for our final round of meetings before the game.

Here it was, the championship game, and I felt like I was going to die.

I slept OK at the hotel Saturday night but got up and still felt awful. I got to the Dome a little earlier than normal, about six hours before the game. At the stadium, I had to do something. I got two bags of IVs and then a Toradol shot just to try to feel better. I wore a sweatshirt to ease the chills. And all I kept thinking was, "Here we are in the NFC championship, and I couldn't feel any worse."

I have great respect for Brett Favre and not just because the Vikings quarterback grew up in Kiln, Mississippi, as a big Saints fan. Truly, he's one of the top two or three quarterbacks ever to play this game. Earlier in the year, when Brett was trying to decide whether to play another season, he and I exchanged some texts. I gave him my two cents about playing until you can't play anymore.

"You still have the talent and the ability and the arm strength," I told him. "If you still have the fire, why not?"

He made the decision to come back. And periodically during the year, I might get a text from him or I'd text him. "Great job . . . Nice game." Just friendly stuff. We followed each other's teams. And now the Saints and the Vikings were playing one another for the championship, and Brett was the opposing quarterback.

It might surprise some people that the head coach of one team would think of the opposing quarterback as a friend of his. What can I say? It's a small industry.

When I saw Brett before the game, we bumped fists but

that's all. "Look, I'm sick," I said to him. "I don't want to give you guys the flu."

He smiled and nodded toward Vikings coach Brad Childress and said: "Go over there and give it to Chilly."

He was joking. I think.

The night before the game, Joe Vitt had spoken to the team. That was fairly common on Saturday evenings. He went through our "keys to victory" for this game.

"Win the turnover battle."

"Be the most physical team."

"Win the field position through special teams."

Ronnie Lott had spoken to the team as well. He'd addressed us in Oakland in the preseason. He was definitely worth a return visit. There was a natural progression to these speakers, bringing the best ones back in the postseason. This was greatest-hits time. Gruden before the Arizona Cardinals game. Now Ronnie Lott.

When Joe finished his "keys to victory," a video came up—loud. Aerosmith was singing "Dream On." And the pictures captured a series of sports triumphs from every realm. Everything from Michael Jordan to Muhammad Ali to the U.S. hockey team beating the Soviets to the Boston Celtics to the Pittsburgh Steelers—this video really captured the essence of sports. We wanted to put ourselves in that winning company.

Red Auerbach and the Celtics. Jim Valvano at NC State. The U.S. Olympic runners. It went on a while, maybe fifteen minutes, with Aerosmith blasting through the hotel meeting room. It was magnificent. When the video was over, it was totally quiet in the room. Ronnie Lott stood up.

Ronnie, a Hall of Fame cornerback and safety with the

San Francisco 49ers, was one of the best defensive backs ever to play the game. A first-round draft choice from Southern Cal, he was known for his pounding-hard hits.

Not surprisingly Ronnie picked up our bat metaphor. As Ronnie stood there he had one of our "Bring the wood" bats in his hand. In his plain, flat voice, he read what was inscribed there: "Bring the wood."

The second time, he said it like a question: "Bring the wood?"

Then he turned to the team and said: "You guys *are* the wood." He recalled his visit with the team back in August. He spoke about winning a championship and what that entails—and how he smelled greatness in the room.

When you look back at that game, Minnesota did a number of things well. Defensively, they played us tough. Offensively, they moved the football. The one thing we were able to do was protect the football and force them to turn it over. We came up with four big turnovers. It was really the main reason we won that night.

Late in the game, they had the ball. Tie score. Brett threw an interception, and now, all of a sudden, we had a chance to go into overtime. And when we won the coin toss, we all felt, "We've got to take advantage of this momentum. We've got the ball here."

The way the game was unfolding, with such high scoring, this wasn't going to be a long overtime. And then we were at midfield, fourth and one, and there was a time-out and a chance for us to discuss the play and make a decision.

Players, coaches, all of us collectively—the question wasn't whether we were going to go for it. It was, "What play are we going to run?"

We ran a short-yardage lead play to Pierre Thomas to our left. If it was fourth and a yard, he got a yard and two inches. As he was going down, the ball kind of came out a little, but he was able to regain control. The officials reviewed the play, and Pierre had possession. He had made a first down.

A huge amount was at stake. But soon enough, it was fourth again. But now we were in field goal range. It was time to put this game in the hands of our kicker, Garrett Hartley.

That's an awful lot of pressure for a twenty-three-year-old kid. To look at him, you might not immediately think: "I'm going to risk my entire season—I'm going to risk the grandest hopes of an entire region—on the power of this young man's concentration and the power of his right foot." He had long blond hair poking out the back of his helmet. He looked vaguely like a refugee from last year's boy band. He could have been someone's maddening younger brother.

He'd had a flawless 2008, going thirteen for thirteen in field goal attempts. But 2009 had not started smoothly for Garrett. He had been suspended for four games after testing positive for a banned prescription. He'd taken borrowed Adderall to stay awake on a drive from Dallas to New Orleans for a preseason workout, not realizing it contained a substance prohibited by the NFL.

We hired forty-five-year-old kicker John Carney to fill in. Carney was like the flip side of Hartley—bald, old enough to be the young kicker's dad, the third-highest-scoring player in the history of the NFL with 2,044 points. Carney handled the placekicking for the first eleven games. Hartley returned in time for the Redskins game and kicked four field goals, including the game winner in overtime. Carney agreed to stay on as our kicking consultant, working closely with Garrett.

But in the late-season game against Tampa Bay, Garrett had missed an important fourth-quarter thirty-seven yarder, sending that game into overtime. Tampa got the ball, marched down the field, scored and won.

But for all that history and all his youth, Garrett seemed remarkably calm as I walked onto the field. I spoke to him for a moment, just the two of us. It's amazing, in a tense and packed stadium like that, how quiet two people can be.

I pointed up to the second tier, to the area where you might hang a retired player's number. Together, Garrett and I looked out between the uprights. Centered directly between them was a fleur-de-lis. These fleur-de-lis were hanging around the stadium. But one of them was right there, centered perfectly between the uprights.

I reminded him that we had good protection with the field goal unit. "How 'bout you hit that fleur-de-fuckin'-lis?" I told him. "Hit your best kick, son. You know why? Because you belong here."

When he did, everyone knew immediately what that meant. The Dome erupted in a positively euphoric roar. We were somewhere now this team had never been before. The Saints had won the NFC! The team and the city were in uncharted waters.

The first person aside from Brad Childress I had the chance to greet was Brett Favre. There was just this minute with him, and this is one of the top two or three quarterbacks who have ever played the game. When I came into the league in '97, my first project with the Philadelphia Eagles was to cut up Brett Favre tape—every one of his scrambled throws. His Green Bay Packers had just won the Super Bowl the season before, in '96. That was my first project on Monday when I walked into the Eagles office with Jon Gruden. And here it was thirteen, fourteen years later—just having played in a championship game against this same player. That really speaks volumes about his career.

That evening was pretty special. When the team was coming back in, we had that Aerosmith song "Dream On" being pumped into the locker room. It was a crazy scene. You had all sorts of people in that locker room. Kenny Chesney. Jimmy Buffett. Jon Gruden. We gave Ronnie Lott the game ball. Avery Johnson. All these people who had been a part of our four-year journey were once again in the Superdome, in the locker room. And they knew the full significance of what all this night meant.

The Saints were going to the Super Bowl to play the Indianapolis Colts.

29

SPECIAL OPS

THE SUPER BOWL CAN be an overwhelming experience for a football team, especially for a team that hasn't been there lately—or at all. There's tremendous pressure to perform on the field, of course. The whole world is watching as you succeed or fail. But there's another battle most fans are never aware of: the equally important struggle for psychological dominance off the field. Like New Orleans and the Saints, the two are intimately intertwined. I focused my attention on preparing our players for the on-field competition. I could afford to. I had Mike Ornstein running Miami special ops.

Mike had no official title with the Saints. His name appeared nowhere on the team payroll or organizational chart. But he played an absolutely crucial role in the Saints' Super Bowl victory, and hardly anybody knows what he did.

Mike is gruff and hyperactive. He paces, and he talks fast. He comes from New York City, although now he lives in

Los Angeles, where he's a top marketing agent connecting sports figures with endorsement deals. He spent thirteen years working for Al Davis and the Oakland Raiders, a time that included three trips to the Super Bowl. Over the years, he's helped several teams handle the complex logistics of America's biggest sporting event. More than anyone else I know, he understands how to get things done in the pro-sports world. He also has a taste for mischief.

It's ironic. Mike was the agent who four years earlier had told me, "Reggie doesn't want to come to New Orleans," and I had replied, "Fuck you." Now he was a close friend of mine and a great asset to the team, flying into Miami and softening up the off-field for us.

I didn't know it until years later, but I'd actually been on the wrong side of an Ornstein pre–Super Bowl campaign. This was after the 2000 season, when I was an assistant with the New York Giants. We played the Baltimore Ravens in Tampa that year. Ornstein was helping our old friend, Ravens president David Modell. All I knew was that in the week before our 34-7 defeat, our players kept grumbling that the Ravens were getting better hotel room freebies. And the Giants' wives weren't happy at all.

That's no mind-set to take into the Super Bowl.

At the time, I chalked up the grumbling to pregame jitters. I had no idea Mike Ornstein was involved. But after the Ravens went home in victory, I heard that David Modell had told Mike: "We beat their ass on the field. Thanks to you, we beat their ass off the field too."

So I'd learned this lesson the hard way.

During the 2006 season, Ornstein had come around with Reggie, and I'd gotten to know the agent a bit. As the Saints kept winning, I told him: "If we end up in the play-offs, you gotta find the guy who did all that stuff for the Ravens."

"I was the guy," Mike told me.

"You were the guy?"

"I was the guy."

Our Super Bowl talk was premature that year, stalled in the slush of Chicago. So we didn't have a chance to test any of this. But three years later, as the 2009 season rolled along, Ornstein and I picked up that intriguing conversation.

We agreed: If we were going to Miami, Ornstein would oversee the nongame logistics. Room assignments. Travel plans. How many tickets Reggie's family might need. If you think issues like those can't erupt into major catastrophes, you've never been involved in planning a Super Bowl. At any moment, a thousand things can go wrong. Much as I admired the skill and dedication of the in-house Saints staff, no one on Airline Drive had ever been through something of this magnitude.

"I'm telling you right now, you're in charge," I said to Mike even before the play-offs began. "Work with our people. But if there's something you want to do that they don't want to do, you tell me."

I don't know all the details of what Mike Ornstein did. But I do know the players and their families were extremely well taken care of. I know the stupid distractions were kept to an absolute minimum. I know we dreamed up a bunch of little irritations to get under the skin of the Colts.

And there was Ornstein with a tiny smile on his face.

The psych-out began with a huge Saints billboard just outside the airport, a solid black background with a giant gold fleur-de-lis. The unwritten message: "Miami is Saints Country."

Actually, it wasn't just one Saints billboard. There were twenty of them in high-visibility spots around South Florida. Mike had mapped out the route the Colts would take from their hotel, the Marriott Harbor Beach Resort in Fort Lauderdale, to the Miami Dolphins' practice facility in Davie. Several billboards sprang up there. Several more appeared along the Saints' route from the Intercontinental to the University of Miami practice field.

Very simple, but very effective. It would be impossible for either team not to notice these signs. The Saints were going to look like South Florida's home team.

When the players arrived in Miami on Monday, I wanted to start off the week with a smile. I thought it might be fun if, as the team buses pulled up to the Intercontinental, I greeted the players in a bellman's uniform.

This wasn't an original idea. I stole it from Bill Walsh, the legendary San Francisco 49ers coach. In 1982, when his team played the Cincinnati Bengals at the Super Bowl in Detroit, Walsh dressed up as a hotel bellman. Some of our players hadn't even been born then. But I liked the Super Bowl association with Walsh, whose team had won the game that day.

The Pro Bowl was also being played in Miami this year. Seven Saints players had made the team: Drew Brees, Darren Sharper, Jahri Evans, Jonathan Vilma, Jonathan Goodwin, Roman Harper, and Jon Stinchcomb. They got down to Miami before the other players did. I asked if they wanted to join my little welcome-to-Florida stunt.

"Sure," all seven of them said.

The only hard part? Finding bellman uniforms big enough to fit the three linemen, Evans, Goodwin and Stinchcomb. A hotel employee named Ana Maria raced in a police cruiser to the home of a heavyset bellman named Bob, who happened to have three spare uniforms he was willing to lend.

As the buses pulled up in front of the hotel, the eight of us were waiting right there. I have to say we looked pretty sharp in our regulation hotel uniforms. We waved as the buses stopped. When the players got out, we asked them crisply: "May I help with your bags, sir?"

It didn't take long for some of the guys to catch on. This was one beefy crew of bellhops. But it did break the tension when they realized what we'd done. Everyone got a smile.

And from what I hear, some of the guys made pretty good tips!

Every detail from that moment forward was designed to make a point.

When each player got up to his room, there was more in there than free stationery and little bottles of shampoo. There was a Sony video camera. There were gift cards from Morton's steakhouse, Subway sandwich shops and Cold Stone Creamery. There was a giant basket filled with candy, popcorn and a week's supply of Title Sports Drinks.

This might all sound minor in the hugeness of the Super Bowl. It was not. I remembered how those Giants players had reacted when they thought the Ravens were getting better swag. I remembered how their wives took every slight so personally—and didn't keep their disappointment to themselves. With Ornstein handling the execution and Mr. Benson paying the bills, I wanted to make sure there was none of that on our team.

We put on extra hotel security. We didn't want the players being hassled in the lobby. We paid extra so the team buses would get presidential-motorcade escorts. Traffic didn't exist for us that week.

And every day, extravagant freebies kept showing up in the rooms.

On Tuesday, it was monster bags of Reebok gear—eight hats, eight T-shirts, two jackets and two sweatshirts. The bags were so big, the hotel bellmen—the real ones—could deliver only four at a time.

On Wednesday every player got a fancy Saints-logoed bathrobe with his name on the back and his number on the sleeve. Thursday it was high-end sweat suits. On Friday, a friend of Ornstein's from Motorola came up with sixty cutting-edge cell phones that weren't even on the market yet. Those were a huge hit.

I made sure the wives were taken care of too. Bathrobes, slippers and extra supplies of designer bath products were left in every family's room.

You knew that, as the week wore on, the players would be out shopping with their families. Or they'd be in some club at night. They'd meet up with Colts players and start swapping stories. Word would get around.

And we began hearing reports: "Really?" the wife of one of the Colts asked. "A Sony camcorder? All we got were caps and T-shirts and a pendant."

I don't know exactly where all this stuff came from. Some I know we bought at a discount. Other stuff was donated by companies that wanted to be friendly—or were eager for good PR. We might have traded some tickets with Reebok.

"Listen," Mike told me when I asked, "if Drew Brees stops in at the local Subway because he got a fifty-dollar gift card, it's the best fifty dollars Subway ever spent." He told me Jeremy Shockey said he really needed two of them. "I gave him mine," Ornstein said. "Guess I'll have to buy my own Subway sandwich."

It was amazing how much difference these little touches made. Ten-million-dollar professional athletes had their dispositions brightened by fifty-dollar gift cards. But all week long I heard from the players about what great stuff they were finding in their rooms and how cool their wives and family thought the whole experience was.

It would never let up.

The family lunches and dinners. The pregame tailgate party on Sunday afternoon. The thirty state troopers ready to drive anyone anywhere. The extravagant plans for a victory party, just in case.

For most of these players and their families, this was going to be the most amazing week of their lives. These were not, by and large, young men from privileged backgrounds. Most of them came from tough city neighborhoods and out-of-the-way small towns, although some had attended top universities.

I wanted the environment to be as confidence-building as possible for our players—and maybe just a little rattling to the Colts.

I wanted our guys to keep their minds on football.

30

GAME PLAN

THE BOLDEST PLAY IN Super Bowl history was supposed to be a fake punt, not an ambush onside kick. And here's something else I'm not happy about. When we opened the second half of the Super Bowl with that game-changing surprise, we nearly ran it in the wrong direction. Had I known the kick would produce a never-ending mosh pit on the field, I probably wouldn't have run it at all.

But thank God I did.

You could call this adjusting deftly to changing circumstances. You could also call it the coach nearly screwing up.

Saturday night, we had our final special teams meeting. Everyone was in that meeting except the quarterbacks and maybe another player or two. Pretty much everybody has something to do with kickoffs, field goals, punts and returns. The forty-five-minute meeting, just on special teams, started at eight o'clock.

"Give me five minutes first," I told Greg McMahon, our special teams coordinator. "I want to talk to everyone. I want them to hear this come out of my mouth."

I walked in and said to the players: "Hey, pay attention. This is important.

"Tomorrow night, when we play this game—and I don't know when it's gonna happen. We might be up ten. We might be up seventeen." No losing scenarios. We would be ahead.

"We're gonna run this onside kick. We're gonna run ambush. And you guys gotta make me right here. You gotta make me right."

The way I said it was more a command than a request.

"I just want to tell you that so you're not surprised when it comes out of my mouth tomorrow."

Originally, ambush wasn't going to be our big surprise in the Super Bowl. A week and a half earlier, I'd gone on a tangent about wanting to run a fake punt. I'd talked to Parcells. We talked about trying to steal a possession from Indianapolis. He had done that in the 1990 NFC championship game out in San Francisco when he was with the Giants. He'd run a fake punt, and it ended up being pivotal in their upset victory over the 49ers. The Giants went on to beat Buffalo in the Super Bowl. I spoke to Greg and Mike Mallory, our assistant special teams coach. They knew I'd been scheming with Parcells. "What's our best fake-punt option?" I asked them.

Nothing's worse, when you're an assistant coach, than hearing that the head coach has been talking with his old mentor and is saying, "This is what I want to do."

I knew what they were all saying to themselves: "*Ugh!* We have a thousand things going on here, and he's talking to Parcells again."

But we spent some time studying tape and trying to figure out what would be the right opportunity, and it really didn't present itself. There were too many variables. Some of the looks were good, but two-thirds of them weren't. The players and the coaches knew I was interested in this. They knew I was pushing it. Yet they also knew enough to tell me what they really thought. At practice, Jason Kyle, our long snapper who's been in the league fifteen years, came over to me at one point. I could just tell he'd been sent by the coaches.

"Hey, Coach," he said, "this fake-punt thing—it's— I don't know. There's so many different looks. It's a mixed bag and—"

"I got it," I said. "All right, I got it. You guys don't want to run a fake punt. I get you."

That was important information. They didn't tell me what I wanted to hear. They told me what I needed to hear. So we began down a different avenue. What else could we do here? How else were we going to take a possession away? Everybody was trying to puzzle this out. I was convinced that winning the turnover game really might make the difference for us in the Super Bowl. The Colts had a very methodical offense. But they couldn't make yardage, and they couldn't score points anytime we managed to snatch the ball. Near the end of the bye week, Greg and Mike came to me. This was Friday. We were still in New Orleans. Greg said, "What do you think about an ambush onside kick?"

An onside kick—not as a desperation move late in the half or the game, but at some point that the other team thought you had no reason to do it.

We had used the play once before, in 2007 against Jacksonville. It was a team that was leading early. We ran the play in that game, the ball literally hit the turf and three of our guys were on it. There wasn't a Jaguar uniform within ten yards.

It was worth a look at least.

Thomas Morstead—our punter, who also handled kick-offs—started practicing the kick. He was a rookie with a powerful right leg and excellent aim.

The technique isn't so different from kicking a soccer ball. With the receiving team expecting a long, high kick ending up back near their end zone, Morstead would have to kick the ball hard to the left, making sure it went at least ten yards past the line of scrimmage. That's the rule. To be legal, an onside kick has to go at least ten yards past the line of scrimmage. But the ball had to stay close enough to us that our guys had a good chance of grabbing it.

I was encouraged by what I saw Thursday, Friday and Saturday in New Orleans. Every time we ran the play in practice, the ball landed perfectly. Morstead could land the ball where he wanted to and do it repeatedly. Anthony Hargrove and the other guys on the kickoff unit were getting psyched. They knew they could beat the Colts to the ball. They weren't even thinking about the possibility of not recovering the ball.

I liked that.

Pretty soon, the players were almost challenging me. "You won't call this," Hargrove said. "You won't call this in the Super Bowl."

Clearly, they were learning to push my buttons.

We were counting on Morstead's technique, of course. But we were also counting on our line. They had to turn and shut up the return. We couldn't afford to be flat-footed at the moment of impact. If we were, the Colts would be able to take a step, react and then it would just be a fifty-fifty proposition as to which team ended up with the ball.

I was looking for better than even odds. Much better.

31

SUPER PSYCH

WHILE MIKE ORNSTEIN WAS spreading Saints gris-gris across South Florida, I was planning my own special ops for the team. Bill Parcells had a few ideas to share.

"Do not wait an extra minute," he said. "Get 'em in here and fuckin' practice. When the Colts are just arriving, you have a practice already under way. You'll be pissing on their turf before they even get there."

It was raining on Monday after the players checked in to the team hotel. I didn't give them much time to play with their fancy new camcorders. We got right to work. In this weather, we couldn't use our assigned field at the University of Miami. It was outdoors. There was an indoor bubble at the Miami Dolphins' practice facility in Fort Lauderdale, near the field the Colts were using. In case of rain, the NFL had decided, the two teams would rotate use of the bubble.

But there was no conflict on Monday afternoon. The Colts

weren't even in Florida yet. They were still traveling from Indianapolis. They weren't arriving until six thirty p.m. We had no competition for the bubble. We had a great practice. The Colts arrived just as we were winding down.

The visuals were perfect. We got exactly the TV pictures Parcells had predicted we would, contrasting images from the Monday before the Super Bowl. Our players, pads on, sweating after a good, hard practice as the Colts were just showing up.

Bill and I had spent a lot of time talking in the two weeks before the Super Bowl. Who better? He'd been there—three times. He believed in leaving nothing to chance. I had asked him, "When we get to Miami, would you speak to the team?"

He was a little torn. He was an employee of the Miami Dolphins, team president. It would be different if he were retired, he said. He was reluctant to meet formally with the players on one team, especially when the Super Bowl was in Miami. Twenty years ago, a guy like that could speak to a team and nobody outside would even know it. Now, with Twitter, bloggers, agents, anything that takes place in this league is immediately known everywhere. Nothing—and I mean nothing—happens in secret on an NFL team.

"I'd like to speak to your team," Bill told me. "I'm rooting for you. You know I'm rooting for you like a son. But I respectfully decline, and you have to understand why."

"Listen," I said. "There's no need to say anything more. I understand. I also know how you feel. Just come watch us practice when we get there."

"Great," he said. "And I may have a message for you to deliver to them."

Bill came with Tony Sparano, whom I'd been with for

three years in Dallas and whom I probably was closest to on that Cowboys staff. Tony was Bill's head coach in Miami now. They came to practice and just hung out. It was awesome having Bill there. He had a chance to watch us. He looked exactly like a proud dad.

Tuesday is always Media Day at the Super Bowl. No practice on Tuesday. So Monday night, a number of the players decided they would go out. They figured this was their chance to cut loose in Miami. I didn't have a problem with that at all. I'm not naive. If I were a player, that's the night I'd be going out. But I'd damn sure make the Tuesday morning bus.

The buses were scheduled to leave the Intercontinental at ten a.m. Arrival time at Sun Life Stadium was ten forty. And five of our players didn't make the bus. There was some question, I guess, about whether I'd told them they could drive themselves. That really wasn't what I had said. Whatever. When the rest of us arrived at the stadium, five guys weren't there—Tracy Porter, Bobby McCray, Roman Harper, Usama Young and Jermon Bushrod. Fred McAfee, our player programs director, was on his cell phone, looking pained. The position coaches were also on their cell phones, trying to track their guys down.

This was the perfect time for a crisis, Bill Parcells–style. It was early in the week. What the players had done really wasn't that big a deal. Monday was the night they were supposed to go drinking. Tuesday was just Media Day. It was all unimportant. Who cares what time Media Day activities are supposed to begin? Believe me, the media will wait. And one by one, the five missing players began to show up. This was going to be a teaching moment. Teaching by confrontation.

"Coach, the league's ready," one of the staff people announced.

"They'll wait," I said. "We're not ready yet. We're still one player short."

By now, Greg Bensel, the PR guy, was getting pretty agitated. Greg Aiello and the other public relations people from the NFL were leaning on him. The reporters were waiting too. The Saints were late. We were still in the locker room. I don't know if everyone knew it yet. But we were going to have a little emergency meeting just as soon as the last straggler arrived. It was Tracy Porter. Finally he appeared in the locker room.

All the doors were closed. I began to speak.

"You guys," I said, starting softly. "You guys remind me of a team that's just happy to be here."

A few players glanced at one another. No one said anything.

I continued. "There's a lot of things I don't do well," I said. "But I have very good intuition. It's gotten me to this point in my career. Part of that is developed. Part of it's innate. But I can, and I do, pay attention. And I have a good sense of what is going on here."

I stopped a moment to let that sink in.

"My intuition tells me you guys are in for a rude awakening this coming weekend. I can smell an ass-kickin' on the way. I can smell a team that looks like they're just happy to be in the Super Bowl. You guys reek of that team."

I could hear my voice getting more intense as I was speaking. I wasn't shouting, but I was personal and direct. I called out a few players by name. I said, "Hell, the secondary— three of the four DB's—can't make the bus on time. Do you honestly think Pierre Garçon and fuckin' Dallas Clark and these other guys from the Colts are out to the wee hours? Late for Media Day? You're late. You're fuckin' clueless. You got no idea."

It wasn't that I was yelling. I don't believe I ever yelled. But mostly, I was just talking to them condescendingly. There was the smallest hint of disdain in my voice. We were now half an hour late for Media Day. Everyone was waiting. The doors were still closed.

I got on the coaches too. That happy-to-be-here attitude was contagious, I said. Too many people were congratulating one another already. We hadn't done anything here to be proud of yet. I had noticed a certain giddiness on the bus rides and in the hotel lobby. "Let me know if you're gonna party all week, because I'll go drink red wine at the Prime too," I said. "We're not gonna get vested in a game plan if this is the way we're gonna go. Ah, hell, I'll go get fucked-up with the rest of you. Is that what we're here for?"

I went on like that a little longer. I think they got my point.

"Before I finish talking," I told them, "I have something else I want to add. I asked Bill Parcells to speak to you guys. You know he means a lot to me. He's a smart guy, and you've heard me talk about him. He's not in a position to speak to this team. He had a message that I was going to give you on Saturday, but I'm going to give it to you today."

Bill's message wasn't something he dreamed up alone. It dates back decades before him. It sounds to me like pure Vince Lombardi, but it probably goes back even further than that. I told the players: "Here's what Bill Parcells said. He said, 'When the band stops playing and the crowd stops cheering—when people stop paying to come—and it's quiet and all you're left with is yourself, you've gotta be able to answer the question 'Did I do my best? Did I do everything fuckin' possible to win this game?'"

I let it hang there for a second.

"And that's not all he said," I continued. "He said, 'I've won two Super Bowls, and I've lost one. There are moments in that loss that taught me more than all the great memories of the two wins.'"

That loss was January 26, 1997, Super Bowl XXXI. Parcells's New England Patriots played the Green Bay Packers in the Louisiana Superdome. "Bill told me this. He said, 'I had replaced one of the special teams players at L3 because of an injury. I had to put someone else in. And just when we had the momentum back in that game—we'd cut their lead to 27-21—Desmond Howard returned a kickoff ninety-nine yards for a touchdown and—wouldn't you know it?—the guy I debated on whether I should be putting in at the L3 was the guy that couldn't make the play. Now that fuckin' haunts me forever, because we had just gotten momentum back.'"

All the successes he'd had, and Bill Parcells couldn't forget the one Super Bowl he'd lost.

"Parcells told me, 'So my message to you and your players is this: You'll live with this for the rest of your life. And so when the band stops playing, when the people stop cheering, when the questions and reporters and all those other things subside, and you're alone, quiet, and all you have are your thoughts—you've gotta be able to answer this question: 'Did I do my best?'"

From the looks on the faces in the Sun Life Stadium locker room, what I had to say and Parcells had to say—all of it had been heard.

"I didn't plan to give you this until Saturday," I told the

players. "But he wanted you to hear it. And you know what? It's appropriate you hear it fuckin' today."

At this point, none of the players said anything. I'm not sure some of them were breathing.

When I finished, Drew Brees wanted to talk to the team, which seemed right to me. Drew said, "Hey, everyone else clear out. I want to talk to the players." So they had their own minimizing. Only then did we do the Media Day interviews.

When we went to work Wednesday, Thursday, Friday, everyone was very focused. No one was just happy to be there.

Rather than holding a phony meeting on Tuesday, the players gave me the perfect opportunity to create a crisis. They delivered it to me in a golden wrapper. The crisis was, *We're not ready, and the team we're playing is doing everything in its power to be ready.* It created a sense of urgency with the coaches and the players even before we began the workweek.

32

TOUGH GOING

THE COLTS WERE A five- or six-point favorite in Super Bowl XLIV, although that spread had jumped around a bit. Most of the media, even in New Orleans, considered us the underdogs. What could be better than that? Going into the Super Bowl when most people are convinced your opponent is stronger? That environment suits me. All the pressure is on the other team.

On paper, the teams didn't look very far apart. We'd both had long undefeated runs in the regular season. We ended up 13-3. The Colts finished 14-2. Both teams had won their respective divisions. For the first time in sixteen years, both teams were number one seeds.

Our offense had led the NFL in scoring with just under thirty-two points a game. Our quarterback was the NFL's top-rated, completing nearly 71 percent of his passes. But the Colts had some advantages too. Their season had ended a little more cheerily than ours had. They lost at the end only when they rested their starters. We'd lost a couple we'd really tried to win. Peyton Manning, their quarterback, had thrown for forty-five hundred yards and thirty-three touchdowns during the season, making him the NFL MVP for a record fourth time. And there was a difference in Super Bowl experience. This was their second Super Bowl appearance in four seasons, our first in forty-three years.

Sunday was a beautiful night at Sun Life Stadium in Miami. Sixty degrees, maybe just a bit cooler. No chance of rain. Very little wind. If you were sitting on our bench, the slight breeze was blowing from left to right. If someone had said, "Dial up the weather for the Super Bowl," this is what you would have ordered. It was just perfect.

That could not be said about the way the game began for us. We won the toss and chose to receive. The Colts kicked off. This being an even-numbered year, the Colts, as the AFC representative, were the official home team, but that meant nothing, of course. Except for this: *uniform colors*. In the stands, I saw far more Saints jerseys than Colts jerseys. From the perspective of our bench, we were playing right to left, into whatever breeze there was.

We had spent a long time planning our first fifteen plays. We call them "our openers." Some weeks we'd go through those plays, and we'd be rolling. We'd score on the first drive. We had been one of the most successful teams in the league on opening possessions. We were first or second in the NFL in first-drive scoring. We went through the first seven weeks of the season scoring on our first possession in every case—a touchdown or at least a field goal.

But this time, we went three and out. So much for openers.

We ran Pierre Thomas. We threw a short pass to Pierre that brought up a third and two. We had talked the night before and all agreed: The very first third down we had, we would take a shot deep. We'd given this a lot of thought. Indianapolis was really a big zone team. They play a lot of soft-zone cover two or cover three. They're a hard team to get the ball behind. They hadn't given up many big plays all season. We knew we'd have to earn what we could underneath the coverage. They would force us to execute seven- or eight-play drives. They weren't giving up a cheap or a long touchdown. They were very well coached, and that was their scheme. But on third down, like so many teams, they used a bit more man-to-man. We saw a little opportunity to take a shot.

So that first third down, Drew threw long. We got the man-to-man coverage we were looking for. But they played it well. Robert Meachem was outside to our right, Devery Henderson to our left and Marques Colston to the inside. Drew threw to Meachem, but the pass was incomplete. It was close. And, hey, we backed them up a bit. But that's what happened. So we punted.

The Colts answered with a quick fifty-three-yard drive and a thirty-eight-yard Matt Stover field goal. *Ugh*. At forty-two years old, Stover became the oldest person ever to play in a Super Bowl. Colts up, 3-0.

Courtney Roby almost fumbled our kickoff return near the twenty-five, but he was ruled down by contact. Lucked out on that one. Brees passed to Reggie Bush for sixteen yards and a first down. But the drive didn't go much farther, and we were forced to punt. Thomas Morstead's kick left the Colts with tough field position at their own four-yard line.

No problem for Manning and the first-quarter Colts.

Joseph Addai's three rushes totaled fifty-three yards. Manning's three completions included a nineteen-yarder to Pierre Garçon for a touchdown. The ninety-six-yard drive was a Super Bowl record.

First-quarter momentum? Solidly with the Colts.

When you start any game, obviously you say: "Gosh, we need to get off to a good start." This wasn't the start we wanted.

The Colts' offense was on the field far longer than ours was. They were converting their third downs, and we weren't converting ours. Jim Caldwell was coaching steady. Manning had been like a machine. We were down 10-0. But we had a game plan. And nowhere in our game plan were the words "Saints fold."

When the second quarter began, we changed directions— left to right now. And we started to get a little momentum going. We weren't scoring touchdowns yet. But it seemed like things might be shifting our way a bit.

Our next drive, which had started late in the first quarter, looked a little more promising. Brees connected on four passes for thirty-six yards, getting as far as the Colts' twenty-two. But on third down, he was thrown for a seven-yard loss by Dwight Freeney. The supposedly ailing Freeney, who'd been nursing an injured ankle, hit our line like a sledgehammer through Chinese drywall. His one-handed sack was better proof of his health than any X-ray. We settled for a forty-six-yard Garrett Hartley field goal and were damned happy to have it. It was something on the board at least. In the final two minutes of the half, we drove to first and goal on the Colts' three. A touchdown would have tied things up. But the run on third didn't get us far enough. Instead of kicking a field goal, I thought we should go for it.

I called one of those check-with-me plays. You run or pass, depending on the defense. They expected a pass. Drew got us to the run, but we didn't gain the yards we needed and didn't score. The only good news was where the Colts got the ball. Their own one-yard line. We held them. They punted, and we inched our way back into field goal range. Hartley hit from forty-four as time ran out. What a run our young kicker was having.

I knew that second Hartley field goal also got me off the hook. People were already second-guessing my decision two minutes earlier to go for it on fourth. Getting the field goal now was some consolation. I still think it was the right call. What you didn't want to do so late in the half was kick off to the Colts, let them have the ball on the twenty and put Peyton Manning in a two-minute drill. The way the game was unfolding, that sounded like trouble to me.

Halftime score: 10-6 Colts.

This was not our finest thirty minutes of football. We were not where I had hoped to be. But we were not out of it at all. Our second-quarter momentum was a whole lot better than our first. Our time of possession was improving. We were starting to move the ball. We were playing better overall. And we were only down by four. It's not like the Saints had never come from behind before. Four points down at the half? That was almost a tie game to us.

That's what I was thinking, anyway, as Pete Townshend blasted into the first chords of "Pinball Wizard" and Roger Daltrey began to sing: "Ever since I was a young boy . . ."—which had obviously been a few years earlier. We had no time to enjoy the Who reunion. We had a busy thirty-five-minute halftime in the locker room. The issue we had was a fundamental one: How could we harness the momentum we'd begun to feel in the second quarter and dramatically expand on it?

The first thing I knew we should do was to keep playing in the same direction. We'd gone left to right in the second quarter. The wind was insignificant. But for whatever reason, that had worked out better for us than right to left. Since Indianapolis was receiving, the direction of play coming back was up to us. It's hard to prove this actually matters, but it can't hurt, right? Why mess with a good thing? I told the captains to let the official know: "I want the same direction as the second quarter. We'll go left to right."

One other thing is important to know here. Super Bowl halftimes are much longer than the usual kind—thirty-five minutes instead of twelve. We had light food in there. I told the guys, "Take your shoulder pads off. Put on a dry T-shirt. We have time here, a ton of time. Rehydrate." Everyone had told us Super Bowl halftimes seem like an eternity.

The players sat and relaxed while the coaches drew up a new list of openers for the second half. Usually, you don't have enough time for that. This time we did. We figured, "Let's put another eight plays up." We made the list. We put it on PowerPoint. We projected it up on the screen, where the players could see it. One by one, I was going through the plays with the offense.

The first one was a play-action pass to Pierre Thomas. The second play was a naked bootleg to Devery Henderson. The third play, we ran it. The fourth play or the fifth play would be a screen to Thomas. But I interrupted myself before I was done. "Listen, we're going to start the second half with ambush," I said. "So when we get the ball, it's gonna be on the left hash mark, the forty- or forty-five-yard line, give or take."

I didn't even want to raise the possibility that the Colts might end up with the ball.

"So you guys gotta be ready for these six plays," I told the offense.

By now, the Who was moving into "Baba O'Riley." I walked over to the other side of the locker room, where the defense was, and I told that part of the team: "We're gonna run this onside kick. How do you guys feel about it?"

"Let's do it," several of them said.

"All right," I answered. "But you gotta be ready now for a short field if we don't recover this thing." It's what Gregg would call a watch-this moment. A watch-this moment is the defense saying, "Watch this. Watch what we do here even though our backs are against the wall like this."

I hated to even raise the possibility of the play not working. But I felt like I had to. We'd be asking these guys to deal with the consequences—the powerful Colts offense starting their first drive of the half halfway down the field. The defense responded exactly as I had hoped.

We were all on the same page now. Everyone was all in.

It was an unconventional move, trying an onside kick so early in the game. Most coaches and football analysts would tell you it isn't worth the risk. An onside kick, they would say, is a desperation move, really only suited for late in a losing game. Almost without exception, that's when the play is called.

When we had studied the play over the previous week or so, we had concluded that the chance of success was north of 60 percent, south of 75 percent. If you search "surprise onside kicks in the NFL," there aren't too many examples. But if you pulled up the cases where it has been used, that's about where the number would land. Those odds sounded pretty good, I thought. But they were a lot more comforting on Wednesday afternoon in New Orleans than they were in Miami at eight thirty on Sunday night. I didn't even want to think how I would explain to a roomful of 130 reporters at the postgame press conference: "OK, I understand the kick didn't work, but let me tell you what I was thinking." That could get ugly fast.

But there was no backing down now.

We'd practiced the kick repeatedly. We were confident Morstead could deliver the ball. We believed our guys could get to it in a hurry. We loved the idea of opening the half with a dramatic in-your-face move. We knew we had to do something to rattle these Colts.

Plus, I liked the unspoken message such a bold call sent to our team. The unspoken message was this: "I believe in you. We are here to win."

33

GAME CHANGER

AS WE CAME OUT of the locker room, there was still some smoke from the Who's performance. The NFL crew was breaking down the stage. The CBS sideline reporter, Solomon Wilcots, grabbed me for a quick interview. I gave no hint about what was coming next. Everything was moving quickly. It was all very efficient. There was no doubt this was halftime at the Super Bowl. And as I walked toward our bench, I noticed a couple of officials getting ready to tee up the second half.

Oh, my God. Something hit me! A horrible thought suddenly raced through my head. "What the fuck am I doing?" I said to myself.

Just then one of the officials came over to confirm the start of the second half.

"Coach, Indianapolis is receiving, and you're heading this way," he said, motioning left to right.

That was the problem right there. If we were trying an ambush, that wasn't the direction we wanted to go. A sharp onside kick to the left would put the ball right near the Indianapolis bench. You'd never want a human judgment like that—who has the ball?—to be made around thirty blue jerseys, the coaching staff and everyone else from the Indianapolis Colts.

"Whoa, whoa, whoa, whoa, whoa!" I said to the official. "Hold on! I want to go right to left! Right to left!"

"We had you going left to right, Coach."

"No, no, no. I want to go right to left. Flip it."

"All right." The official shrugged. And they flipped the direction of play.

I don't know how I could have missed that. At this level in this industry, that would have been a major, major mistake. Never do that! You always want to run it toward your own bench. In the event there's a mosh pit and two or three officials are trying to sort through whose ball it is, the last thing you want them seeing is a sea of blue.

I know I like the Who. I must have gotten caught up in the moment there. What can I say? I'd have been in the coach's wasteland if that had gone through.

The players took the field. Pointing in the right direction now. The official blew the whistle signaling the start of the second-half play.

Here it came.

Morstead hit the kick, and it was perfect. The ball traveled almost fifteen yards past the line of scrimmage.

You have to sympathize with Hank Baskett and the rest of the Colts' kickoff-return crew. This kick was exactly what they weren't expecting, and it was exactly what they didn't want. They certainly acted surprised.

The ball careened off Baskett's helmet and into our Chris Reis's lap. But it didn't stop there. The ball slid down Chris's leg—then the scrum ensued.

Jonathan Casillas was the guy who really made the difference. Just as the ball was reaching the lower legs of Chris Reis, Baskett reached desperately for it, pulling as hard as he could. But Casillas's body was firmly in the mix. He managed to keep several Colts players back.

The whole thing lasted— What? A minute? Ninety seconds? From where I was standing, it felt like two years. I would have waited twenty if that's what it took to end up with the ball. Having ambush succeed was that important.

When the bodies were finally untangled and yanked off the pile, it was our ball on the forty-two-yard line.

Hail, Ambush!

If you doubt the advantage of having all this unfold on our side of the field, look at the replay tape. There are Bill Johnson and Greg McMahon and me and all these Saints players. I'm not saying this was a jump ball. But if it had been a jump ball or anything close to questionable possession, we'd have had the advantage for sure.

Bill had said something similar to his team in the week before the San Francisco game. "At some point, I might just do this, and you guys gotta make me look right." That's empowering. It can't be some crazy, out-there, radical idea. The percentages have to make sense. It's sticking on fifteen when the dealer has an eight.

Credit our guys. They made it happen. And nothing went

as planned. Courtney Roby was supposed to block Hank Baskett. Baskett dipped to his own left. Roby got a piece of him, but not as much as he would have liked. Roman Harper was the primary recovery guy. Chris Reis fell back into that area too. So it wasn't exactly how we envisioned it when we practiced it all those times. But our guys made the play.

34

WINNING TIME

NOW IT WAS TIME to play some football. As flat as our opening plays were in the first half, that's how well our openers clicked in the second.

We started at the left hash mark at the forty-two-yard line, just like we had spoken about. We moved right through our openers—play one, play two, play three, play four, play five, screen pass to Pierre Thomas, touchdown.

There was a whole new confidence on the field—and in the coach.

When you as a coach talk about an onside kick and the eight plays that follow, and then you score on play six? It's back to "Hey, they're gonna throw eggs at our bus in Philly"—and they do. It's just a question of how many. And when the eggs really do hit the bus— Well, it looks like the coach just may know what he's talking about. Instant credibility.

Momentum time! We were just going from right to left now.

We understood. It was going to take more than just an onside kick and one series to beat Manning and the Colts. We certainly knew that. Reducing Manning's opportunities was going to be critical. That fell on everyone—offense, defense and special teams. That's the essence of our team and what made this a complementary game. All three aspects held up their ends of the bargain.

Defensively, we really began to get our stops and came up with some key plays in that second half.

We scored the touchdown off Pierre Thomas's screen. But to the credit of Peyton Manning and his veteran team, they came right back with a seventy-six-yard, ten-play drive and answered with another score of their own. Joseph Addai scooted across the goal line from the four, putting the Colts back on top 17-13. It was a big drive for them. Peyton was outstanding in that drive. Outstanding. Hartley answered that with a third field goal, this one from forty-seven yards, leaving the Colts just one point ahead. Hartley was the first field goal kicker in Super Bowl history to hit three from more than forty yards.

We traded some field position back and forth. Indianapolis attempted a fifty-one-yard field goal. Stover was wide left and a little short. It was still early in the fourth quarter. But it kept them from scoring, and it gave us the ball near midfield.

Now Brees was catching fire. His next burst was a perfect Saints production, seven different players getting the ball, started by a twelve-yard Reggie run and ending with a two-yard touchdown pass to Jeremy Shockey. Shockey not only contributed to us being there. He scored on a play from the tight red zone. His journey's come full circle now. He was healthy and able to play in this game. When he was with the Giants, he was on IR when they won the Super Bowl.

So we scored the touchdown with Shockey, and it was obvious we had to go for two here to extend our lead to seven. At this moment, the score was 22-17. We called a run-or-pass play depending on the defense. The Colts blitzed. Drew got us to the right play with Lance Moore and threw the pass. And in my mind's eye, as quickly as it happened, I thought, "It's incomplete." There was a banter moment with the officials. "Coach, he didn't maintain possession." "Yes, he did." As we were engaged in that discussion, the guys were seeing the camera angles upstairs.

"Coach, throw the flag," they said. "It's a catch. Not a gray area at all." On review, the officials agreed. It was a great play by Lance, a guy who was injured a lot of the season, a guy who we almost put on injured reserve. We'd held out hope his hamstring and his ankle would get better, and they had.

Now it was 24-17 Saints.

Manning mounted another drive, threatening to tie the game again. But a Tracy Porter interception at the Saints' twenty-six—and his seventy-four-yard dance to the end zone—put an end to those dreams for good. After the extra point, it was 31-17 Saints.

Finally, the first real whiff of victory was in the South Florida air.

The Ying Yang Twins had that song "Stand Up & Get Crunk." It was a favorite of the Atlanta Falcons, but we kind of stole it, just adopted it. And every time we scored a touchdown in the Superdome, as we lined up to kick off, that song would come on. And we scored a lot.

That song produced an instant feeling of "Good!" If you were Pavlov's dog, every time you heard that, you thought, "Good, we just scored." It reached the point where Gregg Williams, our coordinator on defense, wanted to hear the song at the end of practice a few weeks earlier. It was playing usually when they were on defense. Offense had just scored.

We'd be out on the field defensively, and we'd still be hearing the end of "Stand Up & Get Crunk." We had played it twice during the week in Miami over a loudspeaker system at the beginning of practice just to get the juices going. Played it loud. But when Tracy Porter scored, we were lining up to kick off, and all of a sudden over the loudspeaker system came "Stand Up & Get Crunk." I thought to myself: "Ornstein! How did he get that done?"

The crowd went crazy. It had to be 80 percent New Orleans Saints fans. Even at the Super Bowl in Miami, we were the home team.

Porter's pick wasn't just a testament to his skills. It was a result of his careful preparation and game planning. "I'd seen it over and over—third down," Porter said of Wayne's pattern. "That was a big route for them to convert on. Through the numerous amounts of film study that we'd done all week in preparing for the Super Bowl. It happened just like I was watching it on film. I made the break on it, and here comes the end zone."

After the interception and the score, we were kicking off, and the defense was back on the field. Were these guys ever going to get a rest?

Thankfully, Troy Evans got a cramp on the field after the kickoff play. He had trouble getting up. It turned out he was fine, but the officials blew it. They gave a TV time-out and allowed the defense to catch their breath.

We got the defense back on the field, but now it was eight minutes later rather than four. And on the very first play, Jabari Greer dislocated his right ring finger. Three minutes left. The problem was Randall Gay had had the flu this whole game. He'd been in and out. Now he was out. He was our third corner. He was throwing up. So Usama Young, who'd moved to safety, was our backup-contingency-plan corner, and he had to go into the game.

So here's your worst nightmare. You're defending this fourteen-point lead, and you're down to a safety playing corner. The clock had stopped. We'd just called a time-out, which was a little unusual. We called time-out and got the trainer and doctor over. Jabari put his hand out. His finger made a due right. It went right at one of the knuckles. It wasn't broken. It was dislocated. Dr. Jones, our team doctor, grabbed this finger—and just jerked it. I almost passed out looking at it. We still were at a break here.

The trainer, Scottie, had been trying to get a splint on the fingers. I looked at him like, "Just tape this thing to the pinkie, and let's go! We don't have time for a splint here."

It was important because Jabari was able to get back on the field. He ended up making a few plays for us. We just did enough to bleed the clock out. Even on fourth down, they went incomplete to Reggie Wayne on our four. There was still this guarded feeling. How much time's left? How many time-outs do they have?

I looked up, and Joe Vitt was coming toward me. I'm saying, "Back up. Back it up."

He gave me a look.

"I'm just trying to hug you," he said. "You're a world champion."

It was only then it dawned on me. "Hey, we can take the knee."

We'd just won the Super Bowl.

35

TROPHY TIME

JEFF CHARLESTON AND BOBBY McCray were the ones who dumped the Gatorade on my head.

I'm not sure how the two defensive ends drew that particular assignment, drenching their head coach with a cooler full of sticky green liquid with ice floating in it. But there's a sudden shock at the temperature change when the ice-cold sports drink hits the back of your neck, then slides across your shoulder and collarbone and runs past your rib cage and belly all the way down to your waist.

I hate to grumble about anything at a time of such triumph. But damn, that stung!

This tradition, dumping Gatorade on the head of the winning coach, goes back to the mid-1980s and the New York Giants—Bill Parcells's New York Giants. Hey, not everything with Parcells's name on it is necessarily good.

I grabbed Greg McMahon. I hugged Deuce McAllister. I

exchanged a "Yes!" with Pierre Thomas. All of a sudden, I was being swarmed by what seemed like a hundred reporters and cameramen, each one assigned to get a different kind of quote, sound bite or B roll—and get it very fast. That's not easy in such a tight crowd. I had a chance to congratulate Colts head coach Jim Caldwell for the season his team had had. He was very gracious. He's someone I certainly have a lot of respect for.

At that point, everything became a little blurry.

Players were coming up, coaches, league officials. "Congratulations," they said.

"You did it."

"Man, that kick was amazing."

"Where's Beth?" I asked the NFL security guy who was assigned to me. I had a thought: "In all this mayhem, I'm not gonna find my family." I knew my wife was headed down to the field. I knew our kids would be with her. But would they be able to find me in this mob?

It didn't take long.

I hugged Beth. I squeezed her. I held her very tightly. She started crying. So did I. Meghan and Connor were hugging us both at waist level and jumping up and down. This was the first time we had been together since right before the game, when we four Paytons had put our hands together and done a little break and a fist pump. From that to this.

"I'm getting Gatorade all over Beth's clothes," I thought. Actually, Connor was even messier. He had his hat on backward, and the sticky stuff was all over him now. Meghan was standing beside him with her broken arm. It was awesome.

"I love you," I said to Beth, mouthing the words slowly so she could read my lips above the noise.

"I love you," she said.

It's funny what you remember from times like this. You know how every once in a while when you hug someone you love, you lift that person an inch or two off the ground? I remember that Beth was up five or six inches with her back arched. It's like an exclamation point on whatever you're feeling when you do that. That's a hug you might give every four years.

The stage with the podium seemed very tiny when the security guy led me up there. Beth and the kids came up for a moment, but they couldn't stay. Drew was there, and Mickey and Mr. Benson, and NFL commissioner Roger Goodell and Jim Nantz from CBS Sports. A couple other people could have fit up there, but not too many. Maybe fifteen or sixteen altogether, no more.

That bothered me. It isolated people at a moment when we all should have been celebrating together the very essence of team sport.

"You got the Gatorade bath?" Brees asked me after tapping my wet black zippered Saints sweatshirt. I don't think he really had to ask. "Hey, we're champions."

"Super Bowl champions," I corrected. "And you're the MVP."

It wasn't the words that made the moment special. It was the feeling, just being there—and being there with him.

Now it was trophy time.

As he carried the Vince Lombardi Trophy across the crowded field toward the elevated stage, NFL Hall of Famer Len Dawson was nearly swallowed in a sea of white Saints jerseys and outstretched black-gloved hands. The players all wanted to touch the sterling-silver football. Their helmets were off now, and many of the players wore white caps emblazoned with SUPER BOWL XLIV CHAMPIONS. From the stage I could see the players patting, fondling and rubbing the trophy as Dawson carried it toward us. Everyone was acting like that trophy had the magic powers of some voodoo charm. Who knows? Maybe it did.

I was still wet, although now I had a white Saints towel around my neck, soaking up some of the Gatorade. The falling confetti was beginning to cloud my view.

When I was growing up in the Midwest, every once in a while we'd have one of those snowstorms with very little wind and flakes so thick it was hard to see the neighbors' houses. You knew you'd have a foot and a half on the ground tomorrow. That's how much confetti there was.

Jim Nantz handed Commissioner Goodell the microphone. Mr. Benson was holding the trophy now.

"Tonight," the commissioner said, "the two best teams in the NFL played another classic game. Congratulations to both teams. Tonight, the Super Bowl belongs to the city of New Orleans, their great fans."

A deafening roar went up in Sun Life Stadium.

"Tom," he said to Mr. Benson, "to you, to Sean and to your incredible team, the hope, courage and inspiration you provide your community is inspiring. So thank you so much. Congratulations. You're Super Bowl champs."

Short, sweet and very, very nice.

Nantz took over from there. "Mr. Benson," he asked, "how can you possibly put this into words, what this night means to you and the city of New Orleans?"

"Well, I tell you," the owner said, "and not only this city but

this whole state. And, Louisiana, by the way, New Orleans
is back. And we showed the whole world. We're back. We're
back. The whole world."

The way Mr. Benson began waving the trophy, Nantz
looked momentarily alarmed. "Be careful," the sportscaster
said. Then he continued. "I know nothing delights you more
than being able to turn that trophy over to your head coach,
Sean Payton."

"I think I could kiss him," Mr. Benson said.

We settled for a hug.

I took the trophy from Mr. Benson. I held it high over my
head. Then, with three strong arm thrusts, I pumped it into
the air. I could hear people roaring with every thrust.

People were cheering. Confetti was swirling. Over my
right shoulder, I could hear Drew's laughter.

"Sean," Nantz went on, "you gotta tell us, your team was
down ten to nothing after the first quarter. And then you had
some of the gutsiest calls—my partner Phil Simms talked
about it—we've ever seen by any head coach in a Super Bowl.
That obviously was born out of a lot of faith in this team.
How did you do it?"

"Well, we talked about it at halftime. It's really a credit to
every one of these players here. There is not enough room on
this stage for all of them. But they carried out the plan. I'm
proud of this team, the coaching staff. And everybody back
in New Orleans gets a piece of this trophy. Here we go."

Drew stepped forward, and Nantz continued.

"And to think that four years ago," the sportscaster said
to me, "you came in. You brought this quarterback over
from San Diego named Drew Brees."

Before the presentation began, I had asked Nantz if it would be OK if I gave Drew the trophy. He'd said sure. "It's time for you to pull off the handoff," Nantz said to me.

I did the honors. I said: "I want to hand off this trophy to the MVP of the Super Bowl, the MVP of our league, Drew Brees. Here you go."

I handed him the Lombardi. Drew and I shared a hug. He kissed the silver football. He too held the trophy high.

"How did you guys pull off this comeback?" Nantz asked him.

I love what Drew said. "We just believed in ourselves. We knew that we had an entire city, maybe an entire country behind us. What can I say? I tried to imagine what this moment would be like for a long time, and it's better than I expected. But God is great. We got the best ownership family in the league, the best head coach, best general manager, best team. And we proved that tonight."

The MVP on top of it, Nantz added.

"Just feeling like it was all meant to be. It's all destiny. What can I say? The birth of my son, as well, the first year of his life. Win a Super Bowl championship. He's been my inspiration as well. So it doesn't get any better than that."

"Congratulations, Drew," Nantz said.

"Thank you," the quarterback said. "Mardi Gras may never end."

We made our way off the stage and back onto the field. By this point, all I could see were white jerseys. There was Jon Vilma and Anthony Hargrove. So many players, so many coaches, so many people I cared about, not nearly enough time.

You know what it was like? It was like being at your own wedding. There were so many people you wanted to visit with—all these people who had meant so much in your life. And I couldn't spend any time with any of them. I was thinking, "Isn't there some way we can stretch this thing out?" I knew that at five a.m. I'd be asking, "What just happened? Who was there? Did I talk to anyone?"

I saw Jeremy Shockey and his mother. He'd scored a touchdown in the game. I remember hugging his mother and just seeing the look on Jeremy's face. Jeremy is someone who is close to maybe four people in his life. When I first signed him, I had him up in my office. I told him to draw a big circle and put in the circle the people who he loved without question. Who did he trust and love hands-down? He wrote down his mother and his brother. He wrote Mike Pope, who was a close friend and coach of his. That day, I told him, "I want to be in that circle."

When I saw him on the field with his mom, that conversation came right back to me. "Thanks for letting me in your circle," I said to him.

I saw Reggie Bush with his girlfriend, Kim, and her mother. I hugged Reggie—he's heavier than Beth is—and lifted him an inch or two off the ground.

"Thank you, thank you—I didn't know at first," Reggie said. "God had a plan, and I just needed you to help me see it."

I wanted to take the trophy back to the locker room. I was eager to get out of that sticky sweatshirt, and most of the players were already heading back there. But Drew and I had to do a few quick interviews. The NFL security guy led us to a golf cart, which whisked us to the media tent. Each of us answered a few questions and then it was on to the locker room.

The feeling in there was absolutely amazing. The catering left something to be desired.

On Tuesday I had told Mike Ornstein I wanted champagne in the locker room, which is actually against NFL rules. Over the years, champagne celebrations had given way to confetti. Gatorade was introduced. At some point, players started pulling Super Bowl Champion T-shirts over their shoulder pads. I've never been a fan of that.

So customs had changed, but we'd all grown up with a certain image in our heads. Red Auerbach, Mike Ditka—when they won something special, they celebrated, really celebrated, with shaken bottles of champagne. Were we really going to win the Super Bowl without a proper locker room toast? Weren't we the *New Orleans* Saints?

"We're good with the champagne, right?" I had asked Ornstein several times during the week. "It's gonna be cold, right? I'm ready to pay the fine." I couldn't have been clearer. "I don't want warm champagne. And I want enough so that we can drink it and squirt each other with it. I want champagne."

Well, I guess he spoke to Mickey about it, and Mickey said, "Listen, I don't know." And the two of them proceeded to "yes" me the rest of the week.

"Oh, yeah," Ornstein said.

"Oh, yeah," Mickey agreed.

I got back to the locker room with the trophy, and there was no champagne. Ornstein had failed me. He will never hear the end of this.

Most of the players got there before I did. Some had already showered. Some hadn't. They were in various stages of semi-dress, shouting and congratulating one another. "I love you, man," they said over and over again. They were laughing and pushing and shoving the way only football players do. I

hugged Dan Simmons, our equipment guy, who's been with
the Saints for forty-three years—longer than Mr. Benson,
longer than anyone. He had a Super Bowl win now.

There were all these people I saw every day—people I'd
have invited to my wedding if I had known them then—all
looking like they'd just been delivered to somewhere they
never imagined they'd be. The head trainer, Scottie Patton.
The equipment guy.

There was one little orange cooler of Michelob Ultra in
the locker room. Maybe there were thirty-five beers in there.
I showered, dumped the sticky sweatshirt and put on my
suit. Finally it was time to make our way to the hotel, where
I knew we had a great victory party waiting for us. Someone
grabbed the little cooler. I had the trophy. We headed outside
to the parking lot. Our four usual buses were ready to go.

As always, I got on Bus One. I was in what would be
seat 1A, first row by the window. Joe Vitt sat next to me.
Brees was right behind us. Greg McMahon, Joe Lombardi,
the other coaches and players—all of them sat where they
always did. Bus Two had its group, Bus Three and so on.

That little orange cooler was in the aisle. The beers were
passed from row to row. You could hear the caps twisting
off the bottles. I think I smelled cigar smoke coming from
the back. Almost immediately, the bus was whizzing down
the highway toward the Intercontinental.

It got quiet in there. It felt almost like that scene in *The
Shawshank Redemption* in which the prisoners are all together
for what they are certain is the very last time. It's not so different for a football team that has just won the Super Bowl.

When you're at the Super Bowl, you get the presidential-
level police escort. The traffic was pushed entirely over to the

right-hand side of the road. The cars were totally stopped as we passed. We were the only traffic.

It was just me and my guys after winning the Super Bowl, heading back to our hotel.

The bus ride was almost silent. Guys were talking, but softly. We had our beers. We had our victory. We had one another. We had nothing to prove and nowhere unpleasant to go.

I had no film to grade. No injury reports to review. No game plan to tease out for next Sunday. We had set a goal for ourselves, and we had reached it together. We had been lifted by our city, and we had lifted it too. What else could anybody want?

As we rode, the people in the stopped cars seemed to understand all of this. At least I think they did. They didn't seem to mind at all. We had been the tragic Saints from tragic New Orleans, but neither of us was tragic anymore.

Horns were blowing. There were sirens in the distance. Some people were leaning from their car windows to get a better view. Others got out entirely. A few were standing on their trunks or their hoods.

I can't prove this, but I'll bet I'm right. Seventy-five percent of those people were Saints fans. South Florida had become part of Saints Country. Our story seemed to have captivated people everywhere. They were screaming. They were clapping. They were waving at us.

As we rolled along, Joe Vitt looked over at me in my seat. We started listing all the thing we didn't have to do.

"No depth charts," he said.

"No injury reports," I followed.

There was only one thing we both agreed we didn't like:

This bus was moving much too quickly. This ride wouldn't last nearly long enough.

My mind went back to the night we took the long way home from Dallas after beating the Cowboys. I wondered if we still had time to arrange something like that.

"This is our reward," Vitt said. "This fuckin' ride."

"I know what you mean," I told him. "I wish we were sitting in traffic like those other people. This ride can't possibly last long enough. I could go through the rest of the night."

36

MARCHING IN

IT WAS ELEVEN FORTY-FIVE by the time we got back to the Intercontinental. Was there any doubt we were going to celebrate?

Mr. Benson paid for one hell of a party. Better Than Ezra played. Kenny Chesney came on at three in the morning. The liquor flowed. Champagne was finally poured. Even after a very tough football game, players found the energy to dance. There was lots of hugging and lots of "I love you, man." Basically, we were up all night.

And why not? There was no next game to worry about. And God knows, we'd waited long enough for this. Four years since I had gotten to New Orleans—forty-two years, five months and eighteen days since John Gilliam's opening run. Not that anyone was counting. No, it wasn't easy. And yes, we got it done. In the days to come, the players and coaches would be scattered everywhere. No one could say for certain how many of them would be back the following year. That's just the reality of professional sports today. No team is forever. Each year is a whole new bet. As we toasted the team, the city and ourselves, we knew we still had some celebrating in front of us. No one seemed eager to call it an early night.

About five fifteen on Monday morning, just as the February sun was rising over the Atlantic Ocean, the party was finally winding down. The players and the coaches wandered into the morning for a long, well-deserved rest. Which was nice for them, I'm sure. I wasn't so lucky. Long before the game was played, the NFL had scheduled an eight thirty a.m. press conference so the national media could question the winning Super Bowl coach. Did I mention this press conference was scheduled for eight thirty a.m.? The idea, I guess, was to have the Q&A before the media all left town.

And that would have been bad enough had the press conference been held in our hotel. Unfortunately, it was forty minutes away in Fort Lauderdale.

The Lombardi Trophy was in the bed beside me. I was totally dead asleep when Mike Ornstein was banging on my door at seven sharp. I'd been asleep an hour and forty minutes, and I'd had a couple cocktails and some Amstel Light. OK, more than a couple.

As I'd said good night, I'd told Ornstein, "I'll pay the fine. No way am I making that press conference. There's only so much I can do."

"Look," Ornstein said. "For forty-four years, the head coach has always been there. You're not gonna be the first one to miss it."

That being said, I clearly was not in good enough shape to

be addressing 250 members of the national media the morning after the Super Bowl.

So with Ornstein banging on the door, I pulled myself out of bed and threw some water on my face. He led me to the Town Car for the ride to Lauderdale. It was Mickey Loomis, Greg Bensel, Mike Ornstein, Drew Brees and me. They were nervous as hell putting me up on the podium—and for good reason. But I was the head coach of the winning Super Bowl team. So really, what choice did they have?

So I got up there slowly. I calmly delivered the message I had. I answered the questions. I guess that's where I said those things about sleeping with the trophy and maybe drooling on it. What can I say? I'm lucky I could string a sentence together at all.

I got back in the Town Car and fell asleep on the ride back to the hotel.

The next thing I remember, I was on the team charter flying home. That was Monday. It's all a bit of a blur. Have you ever seen the movie *The Hangover*, where the guy is asking, "How did this lion get here? . . . Where did my tooth go? . . . Isn't that Mike Tyson?" That was Monday for me.

There were twenty thousand people waiting for us outside the airport in New Orleans. I heard when the Colts landed in Indianapolis, they were met by eleven die-hard fans. God bless 'em. I can't prove this, but I'm convinced: We'd have gotten the same twenty thousand even if we'd lost. That might not happen in any other city—fans turning out to greet a losing team. But I'll bet it would have happened in New Orleans this time. There was that much feeling in the air.

We made our way through the crowd and drove home. Beth and the kids were there already. The family charter had left an hour before the team charter did. We all took a deep breath and finally collapsed.

Tuesday morning, we drove downtown for the parade. The Mardi Gras season had already started. The parades had been rolling since Friday night. The city already had that Mardi Gras buzz. The ladders and the viewing stands were already lining the sidewalks. The Mardi Gras Indians were putting the finishing touches on their costumes. The marching clubs were already plotting their routes. Fat Tuesday was one week away.

With the Saints winning the Super Bowl and the usual pre-Lenten craziness, this was going to be a Mardi Gras like New Orleans had never seen.

There are some things this city does amazingly well. New Orleans can feed you. New Orleans can house you. New Orleans can show you a good time. And New Orleans knows how to put on a parade. No one in the world does a parade like New Orleans. It's a whole different thing here. That's what the people of New Orleans do. Once you've been to a Mardi Gras parade, you are ruined for parades anywhere else.

At the Macy's Thanksgiving Day Parade in New York City or the Tournament of Roses Parade in Pasadena, you stand and wave at what's passing, and that's about it. In New Orleans, you dance, you sing, you wear a costume—you make your own fun.

I can't imagine a better way to celebrate a Super Bowl victory or a city bouncing back.

The Mardi Gras krewes usually spend a full year organizing a parade, beginning immediately after the previous Mardi Gras. We had almost two days, from Sunday night until Tuesday afternoon. Before the game was played, there had been some discussion about a post–Super Bowl parade, win or lose, either way. Again, only in New Orleans.

But now the need for a celebration was pressing and real. We wouldn't just be toasting a football victory. This was so much more than that. This was the way we'd wanted it. Not just reaching the Super Bowl. Not just playing respectably. Winning the damn game. Winning it decisively. And then parading in victory through the streets of New Orleans.

The whole city came together to pull this off.

We borrowed floats from some of the major krewes. They don't normally work together, but here they all were: Endymion, Bacchus, Rex, Zulu, Alla, Caesar, Tucks, Muses, Orpheus and Babylon. None of them had to be asked twice. We reached out to some of the very best marching bands. Budweiser sent the Clydesdales. Two F-18 Hornets from the Belle Chasse Naval Air Station offered air support. I don't think anybody said no to us. Blaine and Barry Kern from Mardi Gras World coordinated a thousand details. This wasn't a bale of hay on a flatbed truck. This was a giant Mardi Gras extravaganza. The police mapped out a special route for us. We thought it was only right we started at the Superdome. And we headed off—Beth, Meghan, Connor and I, joined by the players and the coaches, the owner and staff—for the biggest and best parade New Orleans had ever experienced.

The players and the coaches were as giddy as I'd ever seen them. Ornstein was bouncing up and down. We'd spent four years together, some of us, and this really was what we had been working toward. This team. This victory. This city. And these were the people I most wanted to share it with.

To be on this float, heading off on this parade, held in the warm embrace of a hurt and recovering city, riding with these people I love the most—this is where I run out of words.

That feeling? It's truly indescribable.

As we waited to roll out of the Superdome, we'd forgotten something—something we hadn't forgotten since we moved from Dallas to New Orleans and started this journey we'd been on.

We were starving. We'd actually forgotten to eat. I had no idea what we would find along the route.

But this is New Orleans. These are the Saints. Any surprise is always possible.

This time it came from Jeremy Shockey. It was just a little thing. But the little things add up.

Shockey had ordered fifteen pizzas, one for every float. And right before we rolled out, the pizza delivery girl passed one of those pizzas up to our float.

I just looked at my kids and my wife and thought, "We really won, didn't we? Here we are. This team, this city and this family. We're getting ready to go on this parade. We're eating slices of pizza. Hundreds of thousands of people are celebrating with us.

"You know, it doesn't get any better than this."

▪ EPILOGUE ▪
FOLLOWING SUCCESS

THE NEW ORLEANS SAINTS Super Bowl victory parade had barely rolled to a stop when some people started talking about a "Super Bowl hangover." I don't know where that idea first came from, but I'm certain it wasn't dreamed up by a real Saints fan or by anyone else who really *gets* New Orleans. The basic idea of the Saints' Super Bowl hangover was this: We were sure to pay an awful price for celebrating our success too much.

I reject that notion. Emphatically. I am not apologizing for celebrating success. No team I coach will ever be afraid to celebrate success.

But there was still the question of when it would be time to turn the page and get on with the season to come. And it seemed like everyone had advice to share or an opinion on that. "You went to the White House in July," some people grumbled. "Why'd you go so late?" Well, because it wasn't easy to work out the scheduling based on when President Obama was available and when our team could travel to Washington. When we learned we were going to practice with the Patriots in the preseason, we figured we could tie the two trips together—stop in Washington and then fly on to New England. That made a lot more sense than going to Washington, coming back to New Orleans, and then three weeks later going to New England.

There isn't a single date for moving on. It's a series of steps, a gradual process of moving on from being one year's champion to the next year's team—one that requires intensive planning and thought. There was the ring ceremony in June, where we had a dinner and handed out the championship rings. There was the visit to the White House in July. There was the start of the preseason in August, and then the season opener against the Minnesota Vikings four weeks after that, when the championship banner was unveiled at the Superdome.

All that time, as we toasted our successes and prepared ourselves for what came next, we had an unwavering goal: to get back to the Super Bowl.

We knew repeating wasn't going to be easy. NFL history has proven that. Not since the New England Patriots repeated in 2004 and 2005 has there been a back-to-back Super Bowl champion. The last repeat winners before that were the Denver Bronco teams of 1998 and 1999. In the forty-five-year history of the Super Bowl, the winning team has managed to repeat only seven times, and it's rarely been more than one a decade. The earlier repeaters are Green Bay in the 1960s, Pittsburgh twice in the 1970s, San Francisco in the 1980s, and Dallas in the 1990s.

To me, the Buffalo Bills had the greatest achievement of all, going to four straight Super Bowls. They lost all four. But imagine the focus and drive it took to keep going back and back and back. The Bills didn't even have the thrill of victory to motivate them. I'd argue that that's more difficult than winning two in a row. Seven times teams have repeated. But the Bills are alone in what they did.

Repeating is hard for a number of reasons that have nothing to do with any hangover. For one thing, your off-season is shorter. You're playing the toughest teams in football all the way into February—sustaining injuries, psyching yourselves up, giving everything you've got—while the other teams are resting. There are personnel issues. Contracts are up for players and assistant coaches, and other teams are eager to get a piece of that Super Bowl magic. Plus, your new schedule is going to be different as well: More of your games will be played in prime time, before national audiences. That adds tremendously to the pressure. At the same time, all the other teams are gunning for you as last year's Super Bowl champion. Everyone's measuring their strengths and weaknesses against yours.

But we weren't so interested in all the reasons it would be tough to make it back to the Super Bowl. We wanted to figure out exactly how we were getting there.

Returning to the Super Bowl was the single, overriding goal we set for ourselves—a goal we worked toward every single day after we climbed down off those floats. The players, the coaches, the Saints ownership. Even the fans. Especially the fans. Believe me, in the run-up to the 2010 season, nobody within a hundred miles of New Orleans was thinking: "If we can win more games than we lose this year, if we can just make the play-offs, if we can only not embarrass ourselves too badly, that'll be good enough for us." The Super Bowl created super expectations, and there was no ducking them. Our team, our fans, our city—all of us had learned what it meant to be champions. We all were committed to going out and doing it again.

We had to acknowledge the challenges we were facing and commit ourselves to overcoming them. As head coach,

I knew we had to put all that on the table, all the things that made repeating so difficult. I made sure we addressed it right at the start. In the first team meeting at training camp, I put together a very important list. Two lists, actually. On the first page, I wrote down all the things that could prevent our success in the 2010 season: the shortened off-season, the high-pressure schedule, the focused opponents, the rareness of Super Bowl repeats. On the second page, I listed the reasons we would succeed. The number one reason was the men in that room. Our players. Our leaders. The makeup of our team. Our people, I said, will be strong enough, competitive enough, committed enough to recognize the challenge, to come back, to compete and play great football again.

"You are the reason we will succeed," I said to my team in the locker room that day.

I singled out Drew Brees, John Vilma, Will Smith, Jahri Evans—these veteran players who hold themselves accountable as much as they do one another. We had a locker room filled with these guys. They are how we put ourselves in a position to be competitive, not just in the short term of 2009 and 2010—but for years to come.

You remember in the movie *Rocky* how the boxer played by Sylvester Stallone kept chasing that chicken and how frustrated he was by the chase? Then he finally caught the chicken. When you win the Super Bowl, it's like you caught that chicken, and you're so excited—and then you let the chicken go and you start chasing it again. If someone asks, "What do you do after you win the Super Bowl?"—well, that's what you do. You start chasing that damn chicken again. And you'd better give the chase everything. You have to stay hungry. You have to keep the edge. You have to find a way to convince your brain it isn't satisfied.

After the Super Bowl, Drew spent some time with Joe Montana, Michael Jordan, Avery Johnson and a couple other athletes who'd all had the experience of competing again after a big win. When Drew came back, he had a little page of notes from his conversations with these other successful athletes. They all had faced the challenge directly. They acknowledged the difficulty. They prepared a strategy. And somewhere inside themselves, they found the passion to compete again. Not one of them ever said: "Oh, it's just a chicken. I'm not chasing that again."

Nothing's promised in this game. You start each year from square one. What was important as we prepared for the 2010 season was that we faced that fact directly. We didn't hide from it. We didn't think, "Well, we'll just pick up where we left off last year." No, you go all the way back and you start over again.

It isn't totally natural, keeping such a tight focus. The mind tends to wander. Intensity lets up. It's the same danger you face in any industry. That lesson has been learned by coaches, teachers and bosses everywhere. You have some success. Test scores are up. Your salesmen are moving a lot of merchandise. After a real good quarter or a real good year, you have to control that part of human nature that tends to relax after success. "Let me bask a minute. Let me sit down here and catch my breath."

Walk into any car dealership where the staff is celebrating a record sales month. There's excitement and an air of triumph. And yet, on the first day of the next month, the sales manager is standing in the front of the room, saying,

"Hey, guys, we're starting over now. We haven't done anything yet."

Everyone needs to get focused again.

"Look," I told the players at training camp, "the reason it's challenging is because there's something in success that tends to relax your mind. You tell yourself, 'Hey, that'll get handled by the time the regular season starts.' We can't say that. Those little, little, little things are so critical. We will commit ourselves to all of them."

We faced the truth of the challenge head-on.

We opened at home and beat Minnesota 14-9 in a Thursday night game nationally televised on NBC. That was a rematch from the NFC championship game and a super start for us. Then we flew out to San Francisco and won again, overcoming the 49ers 25-22.

Suddenly, the possibility of a repeat wasn't feeling like such a distant dream.

Then we lost a tough one against Atlanta at home, and after barely holding off the Carolina Panthers 16-14, we lost in Arizona. After we had an easy win against Tampa Bay, the Cleveland Browns beat us too, 17-30.

When we hit that stretch of adversity, we knew for sure that this was a new team. It was a different team. The roster was different. The challenges were different, too. We were in the thick of another season. What had happened a year earlier was finally history. We were fighting for our lives.

We didn't crumble. We didn't lose heart. We worked through that patch of adversity and roared confidently on. And that was hugely important. That was the mark of champions.

We had a big win, 20-10, against Pittsburgh in a Sunday night game at the Superdome on Halloween. That propelled us into a six-game winning streak. Carolina, Seattle, Dallas, St. Louis, Baltimore, Atlanta—that last one a case of taking it up to the Georgia Dome for some sweet revenge. That led to the challenge we had at the end of the season, the very last game we played, the one against Tampa Bay.

The game had relevance only if Carolina were to beat Atlanta that same day, which could send us into the play-offs in a far better position, facing easier teams and playing games at home. Carolina had struggled all season. There was only an outside chance at best that they could top Atlanta. Sure enough, the Falcons won handily.

I do have some regrets about not resting more guys earlier in that game. But the fact of the matter was that if we had beaten Tampa and somehow Carolina had beaten Atlanta, we would have gone from the fifth seed to the one seed. Shortly before the end of the half, Atlanta was ahead, way ahead, and we started pulling out our starters. But we paid a heavy price.

We lost Malcolm Jenkins. We lost Chris Ivory. We lost Jimmy Graham. Three important players, all gone before halftime. It's something I still think about a lot: that dilemma of whether to play your starters in a situation like that. The previous year, a lot of people objected to our not playing our starters at the end of the season, thinking that was the way to get some momentum going. As it turned out, that really wasn't the case. We needed rest. And this past year, we could have used that rest and possibly stayed healthier for the play-offs. But our game and the Atlanta–Carolina game were played at the same time, and it sure would have been nice to avoid going into the postseason as a road team regardless of the record Seattle had. I think our players respected that decision. But we weren't good enough that day.

Sitting here now, I am convinced that that loss to Seattle has a chance to be a big reason why we end up back in the Super Bowl. The sting of that loss is motivating, and it really doesn't go away until you start playing again.

We won eleven games in the 2010 season. I think many people felt we were a dangerous team entering the play-offs. I know we thought so. But it felt a little different from the way it had in 2009.

Entering as a wild card, we knew we had to win on the road a couple of times. We believed Green Bay was a dangerous team. And the only way for us to play a home play-off game would have been for us to win our first two and have Green Bay win their first two as well. Of course, Green Bay went on to win those first two games—and more. Playing on the road, we lost to Seattle, finally ending our dreams of a repeat.

We had played with the goal of being the home team in the play-offs. And if you don't think home-field advantage matters, you've never been in the Superdome for a New Orleans Saints home game. A few times, when we haven't been the home team, we've managed to import the roar of our crowd. We had that at the Super Bowl in Miami. We did the same a couple times in 2010. On Thanksgiving afternoon, at Dallas's new stadium, I swear it felt like more than half the crowd was rooting for New Orleans. On the road in Atlanta for that Monday night game of Christmas week, it felt the same way. No, they don't call us the "Home Team" for nothing.

Our fans are very dedicated and very smart. And they are definitely sticking by us. Ultimately, what they want most is that effort, that energy, that commitment. They recognize that even when you give it your all, there are going to be times when you fall short. But that same enthusiasm, that same momentum that we carried in the '09 season, we felt again in '10. With the winning streak and the eleven-win season and some high-profile, big-game victories, their loyalty has only gotten stronger.

Our fans appreciate what they are seeing on the field. Just like they have, we have accomplished so much in five years, and we're looking to accomplish a whole lot more.

That's the bond that connects the fans and the players and the coaches and all the members of our organization. It's what keeps bringing the people out to the Superdome. Partly, it's all that our region has been though together since the storm—from return to rebuilding and now recovery. But there's also a credibility that is tied to the product on the field. The results are hard to ignore.

We're going into our sixth sellout season—the only ones in the history of the organization—with a season-ticket waiting list of more than twenty-five thousand. We're getting 95 percent renewals today. In this business, it's very simple: It's the effort, the product, the success. It's all those things that lead to a decision: "Hey, I want to be there when those guys play. I want to see more of that. I want to be part of it." That's not something that's given to us or any football team. That's something we have to earn every year.

And we have. In the last five years, we've won more games than anyone else in the NFC, the third-most in the NFL. We keep going back to the play-offs. We've won two conference championships. We went to the Super Bowl, and we won. We've built a real winning culture, and we're coming back for more. And maybe we helped to save a city along the way.

NEW ORLEANS SAINTS
2006 COACHING STAFF

Sean Payton (HEAD COACH)

John Bonamego (SPECIAL TEAMS COORDINATOR)

Gary Gibbs (DEFENSIVE COORDINATOR)

Doug Marrone (OFFENSIVE COORDINATOR/OFFENSIVE LINE)

Joe Vitt (ASSISTANT HEAD COACH/LINEBACKERS)

George Henshaw (SENIOR OFFENSIVE ASSISTANT/RUNNING BACKS)

Dennis Allen (ASSISTANT DEFENSIVE LINE)

Adam Bailey (ASSISTANT STRENGTH AND CONDITIONING)

Pete Carmichael (QUARTERBACKS)

Dan Dalrymple (HEAD STRENGTH AND CONDITIONING)

Tom Hayes (DEFENSIVE BACKS)

Marion Hobby (DEFENSIVE LINE)

Curtis Johnson (WIDE RECEIVERS)

Terry Malone (TIGHT ENDS)

Greg McMahon (ASSISTANT SPECIAL TEAMS)

John Morton (OFFENSIVE ASSISTANT/PASSING GAME)

Tony Oden (DEFENSIVE ASSISTANT/SECONDARY)

Joe Alley (COACHING ASSISTANT)

Josh Constant (COACHING ASSISTANT)

Carter Sheridan (COACHING ASSISTANT)

Adam Zimmer (COACHING ASSISTANT)

▪ NEW ORLEANS SAINTS ▪
2006 OPENING-DAY ROSTER

Drew Brees (QUARTERBACK)

Jammal Brown (TACKLE)

Josh Bullocks (SAFETY)

Reggie Bush (RUNNING BACK)

Mark Campbell (RIGHT END)

John Carney (KICKER)

Danny Clark (LINEBACKER)

Marques Colston (WIDE RECEIVER)

Ernie Conwell (TIGHT END)

Terrance Copper (WIDE RECEIVER)

Jason Craft (CORNERBACK)

Curtis Deloatch (CORNERBACK)

Jahri Evans (GUARD)

Jeff Faine (CENTER)

Alfred Fincher (LINEBACKER)

Scott Fujita (LINEBACKER)

Steve Gleason (SAFETY)

Jonathan Goodwin (CENTER)

Charles Grant (DEFENSIVE END)

DeJuan Groce (CORNERBACK)

Roman Harper (SAFETY)

Michael Haynes (DEFENSIVE END)

Devery Henderson (WIDE RECEIVER)

Montrae Holland (GUARD)

Joe Horn (WIDE RECEIVER)

Kevin Houser (LONG SNAPPER)

Jamal Jones (WIDE RECEIVER)

Keith Joseph (RUNNING BACK)

Mike Karney (FULLBACK)

Antwan Lake (DEFENSIVE TACKLE)

Nate Lawrie (TIGHT END)

Rodney Leisle (DEFENSIVE TACKLE)

Jamie Martin (QUARTERBACK)

Deuce McAllister (RUNNING BACK)

Mike McKenzie (CORNERBACK)

Terrence Melton (LINEBACKER)

Lance Moore (WIDE RECEIVER)

Jamar Nesbit (GUARD)

Rob Ninkovich (DEFENSIVE END)

Rob Petitti (TACKLE)

Bryan Scott (SAFETY)

Scott Shanle (LINEBACKER)

Mark Simoneau (LINEBACKER)

Will Smith (DEFENSIVE END)

Aaron Stecker (RUNNING BACK)

Jon Stinchcomb (TACKLE)

Omar Stoutmire (SAFETY)

Zach Strief (TACKLE)

Fred Thomas (CORNERBACK)

Hollis Thomas (DEFENSIVE TACKLE)

Brian Young (DEFENSIVE TACKLE)

■ NEW ORLEANS SAINTS ■
2009 COACHING STAFF

Sean Payton (HEAD COACH)

Pete Carmichael (OFFENSIVE COORDINATOR)

Gregg Williams (DEFENSIVE COORDINATOR)

Joe Vitt (ASSISTANT HEAD COACH/LINEBACKERS)

Greg McMahon (SPECIAL TEAMS COORDINATOR)

Dennis Allen (SECONDARY)

Dan Dalrymple (HEAD STRENGTH AND CONDITIONING)

Adam Bailey (ASSISTANT STRENGTH AND CONDITIONING)

Bret Ingalls (RUNNING BACKS)

Bill Johnson (DEFENSIVE LINE)

Curtis Johnson (WIDE RECEIVERS)

Travis Jones (ASSISTANT DEFENSIVE LINE)

Aaron Kromer (OFFENSIVE LINE/RUNNING GAME)

Joe Lombardi (QUARTERBACKS)

Mike Mallory (ASSISTANT SPECIAL TEAMS)

Terry Malone (TIGHT ENDS)

Tony Oden (ASSISTANT SECONDARY)

Carter Sheridan (OFFENSIVE ASSISTANT/ASSISTANT PLAYER
   PROGRAMS)

Adam Zimmer (DEFENSIVE ASSISTANT/LINEBACKERS)

Mike Cerullo (COACHING ASSISTANT)

Blake Williams (COACHING ASSISTANT)

▪ NEW ORLEANS SAINTS ▪
SUPER BOWL XLIV ROSTER

Adrian Arrington (WIDE RECEIVER)

Remi Ayodele (DEFENSIVE TACKLE)

Mike Bell (RUNNING BACK)

Drew Brees (QUARTERBACK)

Mark Brunell (QUARTERBACK)

Reggie Bush (RUNNING BACK)

Jermon Bushrod (TACKLE)

Jonathan Casillas (LINEBACKER)

Jeff Charleston (DEFENSIVE END)

Marques Colston (WIDE RECEIVER)

Chase Daniel (QUARTERBACK)

Jo-Lonn Dunbar (LINEBACKER)

Kyle Eckel (FULLBACK)

Sedrick Ellis (DEFENSIVE TACKLE)

Jahri Evans (GUARD)

Troy Evans (LINEBACKER)

Scott Fujita (LINEBACKER)

Randall Gay (CORNERBACK)

Jabari Greer (CORNERBACK)

Lynell Hamilton (RUNNING BACK)

Anthony Hargrove (DEFENSIVE TACKLE)

Roman Harper (SAFETY)

Garrett Hartley (KICKER)

Devery Henderson (WIDE RECEIVER)

Tory Humphrey (TIGHT END)

Malcolm Jenkins (DEFENSIVE BACK)

Jason Kyle (LONG SNAPPER)

Nick Leckey (CENTER)

Bobby McCray (DEFENSIVE END)

Robert Meachem (WIDE RECEIVER)

Marvin Mitchell (LINEBACKER)

Lance Moore (WIDE RECEIVER)

Thomas Morstead (PUNTER)

Jamar Nesbit (GUARD)

Carl Nicks (GUARD)

Tracy Porter (CORNERBACK)

DeMario Pressley (DEFENSIVE TACKLE)

Pierson Prioleau (SAFETY)

Chris Reis (SAFETY)

Scott Shanle (LINEBACKER)

Darren Sharper (SAFETY)

Jeremy Shockey (TIGHT END)

Will Smith (DEFENSIVE END)

Paul Spicer (DEFENSIVE END)

Jon Stinchcomb (TACKLE)

Zach Strief (TACKLE)

David Thomas (TIGHT END)

Pierre Thomas (RUNNING BACK)

Leigh Torrence (CORBERBACK)

Jonathan Vilma (LINEBACKER)

Anthony Waters (LINEBACKER)

Usama Young (SAFETY)

JOIN SEAN PAYTON'S HOME TEAM

The recovery of New Orleans and the Gulf Coast remains a work in progress. I am donating a portion of the proceeds that I receive from sales of this book to support the children of New Orleans and the Gulf Coast and contribute to the region's recovery. At Payton's Play It Forward Foundation, we are focused on the needs of the region's children—their health, their education and their opportunities. Beth and I would love you to join us.

Volunteer. Donate. Come for a visit and support the local economy. I know from experience. The people down here will make sure you have fun.

For updates on our projects, partners and events, visit our Web site, www.paytonsplayitforward.com.

See you in New Orleans!
Sean Payton

▪ ABOUT THE AUTHORS ▪

SEAN PAYTON is the most successful coach in New Orleans Saints history. In five seasons, his football accomplishments include winning the NFC championship, leading the team to victory in the Super Bowl, and being named NFL Coach of the Year. His success has lifted the Saints to the top tier of professional football and been a key factor in the ongoing revival of New Orleans.

ELLIS HENICAN is a columnist for *Newsday* and an analyst on the FOX News Channel.